Digital Photography
QuickSteps

Digital Photography
QuickSteps

DOUG SAHLIN

McGraw-Hill/Osborne

New York   Chicago   San Francisco
Lisbon   London   Madrid   Mexico City
Milan   New Delhi   San Juan
Seoul   Singapore   Sydney   Toronto

McGraw-Hill/Osborne
2100 Powell Street, 10th Floor
Emeryville, California 94608
U.S.A.

To arrange bulk purchase discounts for sales promotions, premiums, or fund-raisers, please contact **McGraw-Hill**/Osborne at the above address. For information on translations or book distributors outside the U.S.A., please see the International Contact Information page immediately following the index of this book.

This book was composed with Adobe® InDesign®.

Information has been obtained by **McGraw-Hill**/Osborne from sources believed to be reliable. However, because of the possibility of human or mechanical error by our sources, **McGraw-Hill**/Osborne, or others, **McGraw-Hill**/Osborne does not guarantee the accuracy, adequacy, or completeness of any information and is not responsible for any errors or omissions or the results obtained from the use of such information.

DIGITAL PHOTOGRAPHY QUICKSTEPS

1234567890 WCK WCK 01987654

ISBN 0-07-225861-6

VICE PRESIDENT & GROUP PUBLISHER / Philip Ruppel

VICE PRESIDENT & PUBLISHER / Jeffrey Krames

ACQUISITIONS EDITOR / Roger Stewart

PROJECT EDITOR / Patty Mon

ACQUISITIONS COORDINATOR / Agatha Kim

TECHNICAL EDITOR / Alfred DeBat

COPY EDITOR / Sally Engelfried

PROOFREADER / Paul Tyler

INDEXER / James Minkin

COMPOSITION / G & S Book Services

ILLUSTRATORS / Kathleen Edwards, Melinda Lytle

SERIES DESIGN / Bailey Cunningham

COVER DESIGN / Pattie Lee

To the memory of my loving mother, Inez, and to the memory of Sarah Murphy.

About the Author

Doug Sahlin is an author, photographer, and videographer living in Central Florida. He is the author of 14 books on computer graphics applications, including *How to Do Everything with Adobe Acrobat 6.0*. He is also the co-author of *Photoshop CS QuickSteps*. Doug captures digital photographs for his clients that are used for print, on the Web, and for multimedia CD applications. He edits all of his digital images using Photoshop Elements and Photoshop CS. In addition he has authored online tutorials and written and co-authored books on digital video.

Contents at a Glance

Contents

Acknowledgments

Many hard working and creative people contributed to this book. Thanks to Roger Stewart for making this project possible. Thanks to Patty Mon for keeping the project on track and filling my inbox with chapters for review. Special thanks to Margot Maley Hutchison, agent extraordinaire, for ironing out the contractual details.

I'd like to thank the companies that contributed information, hardware and software for this book: Alien Skin Software, LLC (www.alienskin.com), Andromeda Software Inc. (www.andromeda.com), AutoFX Software (www. autofx.com), Canon USA (www.canonusa.com), ColorVision, Inc. (www.colorvision.com), Corel (www.corel.com), nikmultimedia, Inc. (www.nikmultimedia.com), and MOAB Paper Company (www.moab.com).

Special thanks also go to the models whose photographs grace the pages of this book: Selina Kay, Stephanie Lewis, Lizz Mendenhall, and Diondrea Pinnix. Kudos to triathlete and world-class friend, Cheryl Durstein Decker. Thanks to my good friend Barry Murphy, who contributed time and energy. Special thanks to Bonnie Blake, a.k.a. Lucy, for inspiration, typos, and being a co-founder and card-carrying member of MLC, Inc. As always, thanks to my friends, mentors, and family, especially you, Karen and Ted.

Introduction

Quicksteps books are recipe books for computer users. They answer the question, "How do I . . . ?" by providing quick sets of steps to accomplish the most common tasks in a particular program or technology, such as digital photography. The sets of steps are the central focus of the book. QuickFacts gives you pertinent information associated with the chapter text, while QuickSteps sidebars show you how to quickly do many small functions or tasks that support the primary functions. Notes, Tips, and Cautions augment the steps but are presented in such a manner as to not interrupt the flow of the steps. The brief introductions are minimal rather than narrative, and numerous illustrations and figures, many with callouts, support the steps. QuickSteps books are organized by function and the tasks needed to perform that function. Each function is a chapter. Each task, or "How To," contains the steps needed for accomplishing the function along with relevant Notes, Tips, Cautions, and screenshots. Tasks will be easy to find through:

- The Table of Contents, which lists the functional areas (chapters) and tasks in the order they are presented
- A How-To list of tasks on the opening page of each chapter.
- The index with its alphabetical list of terms used in describing the functions and tasks makes it easy for you to find specific information within the book.
- Color-coded tabs for each chapter or functional area with an index to the tabs just before the Table of Contents

Conventions Used in This Book

Digital Photography QuickSteps uses several conventions designed to make the book easier for you to follow. Among these are

- A in the Table of Contents or the How-To list in each chapter references a QuickFacts sidebar in a chapter.

- A in the Table of Contents or the How-To list in each chapter references a QuickSteps sidebar in a chapter.

- **Bold type** is used for words on the screen that you are to do something with, such as click **Save As** or **Open**.

- *Italic* type is used for a word or phrase that is being defined or otherwise deserves special emphasis.

- Underlined type is used for text that you are to type from the keyboard. SMALL CAPITAL LETTERS are used for keys on the keyboard such as ENTER and SHIFT.

- When you are expected to enter a command, you are told to press the key(s). If you are to enter text or numbers, you are told to type them. Specific letters or numbers to be entered will be underlined.

- When you need to perform a menu command, you will be told, "Click File | Open."

How To...

- *Frequently Asked Digital Photography Questions*
- *Image Sensors*
- *Image Quality*
- *Raw Image Format*
- *Prepare a Needs List*
- *Point-and-Shoot Digital Cameras*
- *Prosumer Digital Cameras*
- *Digital SLR*
- *Researching Your Purchase*
- *Try Before You Buy*
- *Choose Digital Film*
- *Stepping up to Ultra Fast Storage Media*
- *Add Additional Lenses*
- *Protect Your Digital Camera with a Case*
- *Choose a Tripod*
- *Choose an External Flash*
- *Add an External Storage Device*
- *Purchase a Photo-Quality Printer*

Chapter 1
Stepping into Digital Photography

Choosing your digital camera is your first step into the wonderful world of digital photography. Whether you're a casual photographer or a seasoned veteran, you'll need a digital camera with the features that suit your needs. This chapter will help you get started.

Understand Digital Photography

Before you buy a digital camera, you should know a little about their main components and features, as well as some of the terms associated with digital photography. This knowledge will enable you to make good decisions when choosing your first digital camera or upgrading to a more sophisticated digital camera as your interest in photography grows. It will also prevent you from buying a too-expensive camera with more features than you need.

QUICKFACTS

IMAGE SENSORS

CCD and CMOS devices have rows and columns of sensors called photosites. Each photosite records a portion of the image. After the picture is taken, the photosite information is converted row by row from analog to digital.

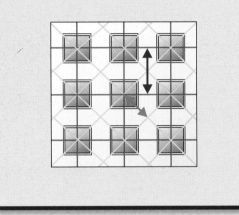

Frequently Asked Digital Photography Questions

Digital technology opens up all sorts of wonderful possibilities. The latest and greatest technology, however, often creates more questions for the user than it answers. The following list of questions and answers will provide you with a basic overview of digital camera technology. As we get into more detailed discussions of camera features and image editing later in the book, you will be able to refer back to this list if you need to.

Q: How does a digital camera work?

A: A digital camera has a lens and shutter just like a film camera. Both types of camera use a metering device to determine the exposure needed to record the image. The conventional camera records the image on film, which needs to be processed in a lab before you see the results. The digital camera's image sensor acts as the film, recording the information in digital format, after which the image is transferred to the camera's storage device. The picture is processed in the camera and you see the results almost immediately on the camera's LCD monitor.

Q: What are image sensors?

A: The image sensor is similar to the CPU chip in your computer in that it processes and stores data in digital form. Digital cameras use two kinds of image sensors: CCD (charge coupled device) or CMOS (complementary metal oxide semiconductor). CMOS sensors are thinner and can accommodate additional circuitry for features such as image stabilization. They also consume less battery power than CCDs. High-tech cameras with CMOS sensors feature noise reduction circuitry, which assures you of sharp pictures in most conditions.

Q: How do digital cameras store images?

A: Modern digital cameras use removable storage media as shown in Figure 1-1. Think of camera storage devices as your digital film. They serve the same function as the hard drive on your computer, without as many moving parts. Storage device capacity is measured in megabytes or, for ultra-high capacity cards, gigabytes—the same units of measure used to measure computer hard drive capacity. The number of

Figure 1-1: *Removable storage media comes in a variety of shapes and sizes.*

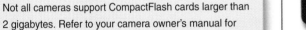

NOTE

Not all cameras support CompactFlash cards larger than 2 gigabytes. Refer to your camera owner's manual for additional information.

NOTE

Storage device types are not interchangeable. If your camera uses CompactFlash media, then that is the *only* media that will fit into the camera. However, there are card readers available that will read different types of storage devices. You can use card readers to transfer images from the media card to your computer.

images you can store on a device is determined by image resolution, which we will discuss later. The following storage devices are commonly used by digital cameras:

- **CompactFlash** cards are commonly found on many consumer point-and-shoot cameras, as well as on high-end digital cameras and professional digital SLR (single lens reflex) digital cameras. They are sturdy and have storage capacities ranging from 8MB to 8GB.

- **Secure Digital** cards are used for information storage on many devices, including PDA devices and digital cameras. Secure Digital cards are available with capacities as high as 512MB.

*Figure 1-2: **A high-resolution image is comprised of millions of pixels.***

*Figure 1-3: **Pixels are squares of solid color.***

- **Memory Stick** is the storage media used by Sony digital cameras. Sony's Memory Stick cards have capacities as high as 1GB.

- **SmartMedia** cards are used by certain Olympus models and are available with a capacity as high as 128MB.

- **xD-Picture** cards are used by Fujifilm and Olympus digital cameras and are available with a capacity as high as 512MB.

Q: **What is a pixel?**

A: Short for "picture element," a pixel is a single point of color in a digital display. A pixel is composed of varying degrees of three colors: red, green, and blue (or RGB). The blending of varying amounts of RGB gives each pixel its distinctive color. On a true color (24-bit) monitor, millions of pixels are arranged in rows and columns packed so tightly together that they appear to blend into continuous tones and create a solid image. The image size in pixels refers to the number of vertical and horizontal rows of pixels displayed on a screen. Figure 1-2 shows a high-resolution image. Figure 1-3 is a magnified section of the image which allows you to see the pixels that comprise the image.

Q: **What is image resolution and how does it relate to image size?**

A: Image resolution is the number of pixels per inch used to create an image. When you work with an image that has a high resolution, you can readily see the difference in quality because the additional pixels make it possible to reproduce subtle variations in color. An image that measures 10 × 8 inches at a resolution of 300 pixels per inch (ppi) has pixel dimensions of 3000 × 2400.

Q: **What are megapixels?**

A: A megapixel, the unit of measure for the number of pixels captured by a digital camera image sensor, is a million pixels. For example, a 5.0 megapixel camera is capable of creating images with a maximum image size of 2592 × 1944 pixels (a total of

QUICKFACTS

IMAGE QUALITY

An 8 × 10 inch image at 72ppi has pixel dimensions of 720 × 576. Images for computer viewing require a resolution of only 72ppi. Good-quality printed images, however, require a resolution of at least 200ppi or, preferably, 300ppi. If you print an 8 × 10 inch image with pixel dimensions of 720 × 576, a resolution of 72ppi, the result will be blocky and unsatisfactory. If, on the other hand, you print an image with pixel dimensions of 3000 × 2400 at 300ppi, you will get a photo-realistic 8 × 10 inch image with smooth blending of color. Most digital cameras have a resolution of 180ppi or better.

Increasing the ISO setting can introduce digital noise, which is similar to the graininess that appears in images recorded with film cameras using high-speed film. Many cameras have noise filters. You can also purchase third-party noise filters as plug-ins for your image-editing application.

5,038,848 pixels). The maximum image size of your camera determines the maximum size image you can print. For example, if you purchase a 5.0 megapixel camera, it is capable of creating a picture with a maximum image size of 2592 × 1944 pixels. To determine the maximum print size, you divide the number of pixels by the image resolution. For example, if the camera has image resolution of 240ppi, and you shoot a picture with an image size of 2592 × 1944 pixels, you can print a photo-quality image that is 10.8 × 8.1 inches. Higher resolution images are larger in file size, which means you can store fewer of them on your camera's removable storage media.

Q: What is an ISO rating?

A: ISO (International Organization for Standardization) refers to the sensitivity of your digital camera. This rating is similar to the speed of camera film. High-end digital and digital SLR cameras enable you to change ISO ratings as needed. When you shoot in normal lighting conditions, a low ISO setting will give you the best results. When shooting in low light conditions, choosing a higher ISO setting makes the camera more sensitive, enabling you to capture images in low light settings without using a tripod. The ratings range from ISO 50 (slow) to ISO 3200 (high).

Q: What are image file formats?

A: When your digital camera processes an image, it takes the data from the image sensor and compresses it into the format you specify. The file format you specify combined with the image size determines the file size and therefore the amount of room needed on your camera's removable storage device. Most digital cameras use the JPEG (Joint Photographic Experts Group) and/or TIFF (Tagged Information File Format) file formats. TIFF files offer the best image quality, while JPEG images are compressed to a higher degree, resulting in smaller file sizes. Many digital cameras have a setting for image quality, the choices being fine and normal. High-quality images result in higher file sizes and sharper pictures.

Q: **What camera features do I need?**

A: The answer to this question depends on how you're going to use the camera. If you're a casual picture taker, you can probably get by with a point-and-shoot digital camera. Even the most basic point-and-shoot digital camera has different shooting modes, and many come with features such as red-eye reduction. Basic point-and-shoot digital cameras generally offer 3 megapixel quality, which means you can get good-quality 3 × 5 inch images from the camera. However, if you're going to take a wide variety of pictures and want the most from your digital camera, you'll be happier with a high-end digital camera with a built-in wide angle to telephoto zoom lens or a digital SLR. The following are a few features found on high-end cameras that you may want to consider:

- **Auto exposure bracketing (AEB)** enables you to take three pictures of a scene, one with the camera's recommended setting, one with a higher exposure, and one with a lower exposure. This option ensures you'll get the shot, even in difficult lighting conditions.

- **Movie mode** enables you to create movies with your digital camera. While a camera with movie mode is not a substitute for a digital video camera, this feature will enable you to create movies that can be viewed with the associated software on a computer monitor or from a website. Most digital cameras offer a movie mode that lets you create a movie at 15fps (frames per second). The length of the movie you can capture depends on the camera firmware. If your camera movie mode offers uninterrupted video, the length of the movie is determined by the size of your memory card. Other cameras have a maximum of three minutes per recorded movie. Some cameras have built-in microphones that enable you to create a movie with sound.

- **Macro mode** enables you to take close-up images of objects such as flowers, jewelry, and watches.

- **Through-the-lens focusing** uses an electronic viewfinder that displays what the camera image sensor records.

- **Optical zoom of 5X or more** enables you to zoom in tight on a scene, which is useful when photographing wildlife from afar. A high level of optical zoom is the equivalent of having a 35mm telephoto lens with a focal length of 180mm or greater. For example, a Canon S1 IS camera lens has a maximum optical zoom of 10X, which is the 35mm equivalent of a 380mm lens.

- **Image stabilization** compensates for any operator movement while the camera is recording the image. Image stabilization helps you get a sharper image when you're

TIP

If you're considering a camera with through-the-lens focusing, point the camera toward a bright light source and view the scene through the viewfinder. Some cameras with through-the-lens focusing don't do a good job of displaying a brightly lit scene through the electronic eyepiece.

CAUTION

If you need a digital camera that's capable of zooming in tightly on a scene, always opt for a high degree of *optical* zoom. Many cameras offer *digital* zoom to augment the maximum focal length of the camera lens. When a camera is in digital zoom mode, however, the camera magnifies a small portion of the image as recorded in maximum optical zoom and then expands the image to a larger size, which results in a blockier image because there are fewer pixels.

QUICKFACTS

RAW IMAGE FORMAT

RAW image format is available on many high-end digital cameras. When you capture images in RAW format, you capture the digital data initially recorded by your camera image sensor with no additional processing or compression. The amount of data in a RAW image results in a larger file size, but the RAW format gives you a wider range of color with which to work. Images captured in RAW format have dazzling color and fine detail. Cameras capable of recording images in RAW format include software that enables you to process the image after downloading it to your computer. After processing the image, you can export it as a TIFF or JPEG file for further editing in your image-editing application. The data captured by your camera in RAW mode enables you to create dazzling photographs like the one shown in the following image. Once the domain of high-end users only, the RAW format is increasingly becoming an option for all levels of digital camera owners to consider in the proper circumstances, as we will discuss in Chapter 3.

using maximum zoom. This option is especially useful on cameras with an optical zoom of 5X or greater.

- **Exposure control** enables you to capture images in aperture priority mode or shutter priority mode, depending on the type of scene you are capturing. Many cameras also give you the option of setting exposure manually. When you shoot in aperture priority mode, you can control how much of the scene is in focus (known as depth of field). When you shoot in shutter priority mode, the camera exposes the image based on the shutter speed you specify. A high shutter speed enables you to freeze action. If your camera has a manual mode, you set both shutter speed and aperture to arrive at the desired exposure.

Q: How do I get the images into my computer?

A: You can download the images from your camera to your computer using the USB cable supplied with most modern digital cameras, which you connect to a USB slot on

your computer. Alternatively, you can purchase a card reader, which is also hooked to your computer via a USB cable, as shown in Figure 1-4. When you connect your digital camera to a computer or insert a memory card into a card reader that's connected to your computer, the computer recognizes the device, and you can download the images to the desired folder on your hard drive. After you download the images to your computer, you can edit them in your image-editing application to prepare them for viewing or optimize them for printing.

*Figure 1-4: **You can download images to your computer using a card reader.***

Purchase a Digital Camera

Whether you're going to purchase your first digital camera or purchase a second digital camera with more powerful features, it's a good idea to do your homework first. If you rush out blindly and buy the first digital camera that looks cool or the one the friendly salesperson recommends, you may end up with a bad case of buyer's remorse when you actually use the camera.

Prepare a Needs List

Digital cameras are hot ticket items, and there are all manner of makes and models available. If you prepare a list of your needs before shopping for your camera, you'll get exactly what you want and not succumb to slick advertising claims. If you buy a digital camera without knowing what you really need, you'll end up with either a camera that falls short of the mark, or a high-priced camera with bells and whistles you'll never use. Prepare your list by answering the following questions:

- **How often will you use the camera and what type of photographs will you take?** If you use a camera infrequently to capture only images of friends and family events, your best bet may be a point-and-shoot digital camera.

- **Will you be using the camera for wildlife photography?** If so, consider a model with a 5X or greater optical zoom. Another useful feature for wildlife photography is a camera that will shoot several frames per second.

- **Will you be photographing sporting events?** If so, your camera should have a sports shooting mode or allow you to select a shooting mode that gives you the option of setting the shutter speed, which enables you to freeze action such as athletes in motion.

- **Will you be photographing portraits of people?** If so, your camera needs a portrait mode. Better yet, the camera should have an aperture-preferred shooting mode and a fast telephoto lens with an aperture setting of f/2.8, which enables you to create a limited depth of field where your subject is in clear focus, but the background and foreground are blurry.

- **Do you own a 35mm SLR camera manufactured by Canon or Nikon?** If so, your auto focus (AF) lenses may work with the manufacturer's digital SLR.

- **Do you want the capability of editing your images after downloading them to your computer?** If so, your camera should include image-editing software. If the camera has Adobe Photoshop Elements, JASC Paint Shop Pro, or similarly powerful software, you can use these applications to color-correct, resize and crop images, and much more.

- **Do you want the capability of printing photo-quality prints of your images?** If so, your camera should be 3.2 megapixels or greater. A 3.2 megapixel camera in best

NOTE

A digital SLR (single lens reflex) camera uses a movable mirror and an optical pentaprism to direct the light from the lens to the viewfinder. Therefore you see the scene exactly as it will appear in your photograph. When you press the shutter button, the mirror flips up and the light is directed towards the image sensor.

NOTE

Many cameras ship with proprietary software that doesn't give you a lot of power when it comes to editing images. The image-editing applications that will be discussed in the later part of this book can be purchased from retail outlets and online.

2 3 4 5 6 7 8 9 10

shooting mode will give you high-quality 4 × 6 inch prints; a 5.0 megapixel or better camera will yield images as large as 8 × 10 inches.

- **Will you be shooting in low light?** If so, your camera should offer the option to set the ISO rating. The camera should also have a setting of ISO 400 or better.

- **Are you an experienced photographer?** If so, you're likely to shoot subjects that are backlit. In this regard, your camera should have a mode for shooting in backlit situations. Better yet, the camera should have multiple metering modes.

- **Will you be capturing images of fast-moving objects?** If so, your camera should have a maximum shutter speed of 1/2000 of a second or more.

- **Do you want the capability of taking wide angle or telephoto shots beyond the range of the camera lens?** If so, your camera should have some method of accepting accessory lenses. Many high-end digital cameras have lens threads that enable you to attach an auxiliary wide-angle or telephoto lens. If you purchase a digital SLR camera, you can choose from a wide variety of manufacturer and after-market lenses in a wide range of focal lengths.

Know Your Choices

After assessing your needs, the next step is to find the ideal camera with features to suit your needs and lifestyle. There are many types of digital cameras, and each type of camera has a plethora of models by various manufacturers. Figure 1-5 shows a few of the different types of digital cameras available from Canon. The following sections will give you an idea of the types of cameras that are available today.

Point-and-Shoot Digital Cameras

If you take pictures infrequently but would still like the convenience of a digital camera, a point-and-shoot camera is ideal for you. Point-and-shoot cameras are relatively easy to operate, and many feature optical zoom up to 2X. Some feature multiple shooting modes to compensate for lighting conditions and fast-moving objects. Most point-and-shoot cameras do not have a through-the-lens viewfinder. In this category, you'll find cameras that are small enough to fit in your shirt pocket, from low megapixel cameras capable of creating wallet-sized

*Figure 1-5: **Each camera manufacturer offers a wide array of digital cameras.***

TIP

Many cameras have a hard time focusing in low light situations. You can overcome this obstacle by choosing a camera that gives you the ability to focus manually.

UICKSTEPS

RESEARCHING YOUR PURCHASE

After creating your list, you'll have the necessary information to search for a digital camera that matches your needs. After you find a camera that matches your needs, you may feel you're ready to purchase the camera. However, camera manufacturers have different ways of incorporating features with their products. Some implementations are innovative, while others fall far short of the mark. Before buying a camera, it's always a good idea to read what the experts have to say about the model.

With the information from your needs list, you're ready to find a camera that includes the desired features. Visit websites that provide news and reviews about current camera models.

A couple of good websites to check out for this type of information are www .dpreview.com and www.cnet.com. This illustration shows an authoritative camera review from www .dpreview.com.

You can also visit your favorite search

Continued . . .

prints up to 5-megapixel cameras that enable you to create 4 × 6 inch prints. These cameras generally retail for less than $300.

Prosumer Digital Cameras

If you're the creative type that likes to take pictures you can frame and share with relatives and friends, consider purchasing a "prosumer" camera. Cameras in this category feature extended zoom lenses that enable you to creatively compose your scene and zoom in on faraway objects. Many cameras in this category feature through-the-lens viewing, which enables you to accurately compose a scene. Most cameras in this category feature multiple shooting modes, which you can use to control how much of the scene is in focus and to freeze action. Prosumer cameras with a built-in zoom and through-the-lens viewfinders are often referred to as zoom lens reflex cameras. Cameras in this category begin at the 3.2 megapixel level and retail for between $500 and $1000.

Digital SLR

If you're an advanced hobbyist or a professional photographer making the switch to digital, a digital SLR is the logical camera to choose. Digital SLRs function just like their film-carrying brethren. In fact, if you currently own a 35mm SLR, you may be able to use your current lenses with a digital SLR by the same manufacturer. Digital SLRs feature interchangeable lenses, on-camera flash, and advanced shooting modes that you can use to creatively photograph the world around you. You can accessorize your camera by purchasing lenses, filters, off-camera flashes, and more. These cameras range in price from $999 to $4500.

TIP

You can also find digital camera reviews in photography magazines. In fact, many magazines contain nothing but information and reviews about popular digital cameras and accessories. Your local bookstore probably has a section devoted to photography magazines.

TIP

If you're previewing the camera in a computer superstore, ask the salesperson to download the images to a computer and preview them onscreen.

Search for the Perfect Camera

The choice of which camera to use is highly subjective. You may be inclined to make your purchase as soon as you've completed your needs list and selected the ideal candidate after reading online reviews. You may also be tempted to find the lowest price online and order the camera direct. Even though the camera has the features you need and has received glowing reviews, however, it may not be the right camera for you.

Try Before You Buy

The only way you can be sure if your candidate is indeed the ideal digital camera for you is to hold it in your hands and make sure the controls are comfortable, the camera is easy to use, and it takes acceptable pictures. In other words, the only way you really can be sure that the camera is right for you is to try before you buy. Visit a local retailer that stocks your ideal camera. Ask the salesperson to let you hold the camera. Look through the viewfinder and press the shutter button halfway. Notice how quickly the camera focuses on the subject. If the camera is slow to respond, or if it takes a second or two to focus, you may end up losing spontaneous shots.

Press the shutter button all the way to take a picture. Notice how long it takes the camera to record the picture. Most digital cameras have shutter lag (the time it takes to record the picture after you press the shutter button) to some degree. However, if the lag is excessive, you run the risk of not capturing spontaneous images.

Put the camera through its paces by taking pictures of objects in the store. Use the camera zoom and flash to see how they perform. Review the pictures you've just taken using the camera's built-in LCD monitor. Make sure the images are sharp and colorful. (The only true test of image quality is to view it on a computer screen, but the LCD monitor may give you an idea of what the camera is capable of.)

QUICKFACTS

STEPPING UP TO ULTRA FAST STORAGE MEDIA

If you own a high-end digital camera capable of recording multiple frames with other features such as auto exposure bracketing, you may find that a standard memory card isn't up to the task. Standard memory cards were designed for point-and-shoot cameras. The read and write speed of a standard memory card may not be fast enough to keep up with your high-end camera. When a memory card can't write the information fast enough, the data is stored in the camera's memory buffer and written to the memory card when available. You will not be able to record images when the camera's memory buffer is full.

If your camera uses CompactFlash, Memory Stick, or Secure Digital media, you'll be able to equip your camera with a fast memory card. SanDisk (www.sandisk .com) is one of many manufacturers that offers a line of professional memory cards. Sony offers fast media storage in the form of Memory Stick Pro for users of Sony digital cameras. The following illustration shows some of the high-performance memory cards you can purchase at your local retailer or online.

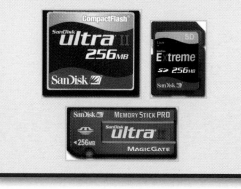

Choose Digital Film

Your camera's removable storage media is the digital equivalent of film. Most manufacturers include one removable storage media card with the camera, which, when the card is full of images, you can download to your computer. However, if you shoot lots of pictures when you travel and don't have access to a computer, you'll need additional cards.

The size of the digital media and the image quality you choose determines how many images you can store. Some media storage devices have capacities as high as 2GB. If you own a high-end digital SLR that uses CompactFlash media, you may be able to benefit from the new super-size storage devices with capacities up to 8GB. The following table shows the number of images you can fit on a 128MB CompactFlash card. The information in Table 1-1 is based on a 6.3 megapixel Canon camera.

TABLE 1-1: *Image Capacity for 128MB CompactFlash Card*

IMAGE SIZE/ QUALITY	IMAGE SIZE (PIXELS)	FILE FORMAT	COMPRES-SION	FILE SIZE	CAPACITY
Large/fine	3072 × 2048	JPEG	Low	2.4MB	50 images
Large/normal			High	1.2MB	103 images
Medium/fine	2048 × 1360		Low	1.3MB	95 images
Medium/normal			High	0.7MB	184 images
Small/fine	1536 × 1024		Low	0.8MB	145 images
Small/normal			High	0.4MB	282 images

Accessorize Your Camera

When you purchase a point-and-shoot or high-end digital camera, you get just enough equipment to take pictures. When you purchase a digital SLR, you often get just the body. Some retailers offer digital SLR kits that include a lens and perhaps a flash. Whatever type of camera you buy, you may find that you want to add a case, a tripod, or other items to improve the quality of your experience and the photos you take.

Add Additional Lenses

If you own a high-end digital camera, you can purchase a wide angle or telephoto attachment to extend your picture taking capabilities. High-end digital cameras usually feature accessory threads at the end of the lens. You simply screw the attachment into the threads and take your picture. If you own a digital SLR, the sky's the limit. You can choose from a wide range of lenses supplied by the camera manufacturer or third-party lens manufacturers. You can purchase lenses from a local retailer or through Internet outlets. It's a good idea to try the lens before buying, especially if you're buying a lens manufactured by a third-party lens manufacturer. Figure 1-6 shows lenses for a Canon digital SLR.

NOTE

Digital camera image sensors are not the same size as 35mm film. Therefore 35mm lenses do not act the same on a digital SLR. A digital SLR has a magnification ratio based on the difference in size between the camera image sensor and the frame size of 35mm film. Most digital SLR cameras have a magnification ratio of 1.5 or 1.6. Therefore, a 20mm lens mounted on a digital camera performs like a 32mm (20 × 1.6) lens on a 35mm camera.

TIP

If you purchase products online, be sure the retailer has a good reputation. You can find out information about Internet retailers at http://www.resellerratings.com/.

*Figure 1-6: **Accessorize your digital SLR with additional lenses.***

Figure 1-7: *Protect your investment with a camera case.*

Protect Your Digital Camera with a Case

If you own a small point-and-shoot camera, you may be able to get by without a case. After all, most of them are small enough to fit in a shirt pocket. However, if you own a high-end digital camera or a digital SLR, you'll need space to store the camera and your accessories. A case also serves as protection when the weather is inclement.

When you purchase a case for your camera, choose one that is large enough for the camera and the accessories you now own, as well as accessories that you are considering purchasing in the near future. You can purchase a camera case from a well-stocked retail outlet, a camera store, or an online camera store. Some camera cases are customizable with removable partitions that attach to the case with Velcro. Figure 1-7 shows examples of camera cases for digital cameras.

Choose a Tripod

Most point-and-shoot digital cameras feature a tripod thread, and all high-end zoom lens reflex and digital SLR cameras have one. This enables you to secure the camera to a tripod. A tripod steadies the camera when you're taking a picture that requires a lengthy exposure. Figure 1-8 shows a tripod suitable for a lightweight digital camera.

If you own a digital SLR, note the weight of your camera before you purchase a tripod. (This isn't mandatory when you're buying a tripod for a point-and-shoot or lightweight high-end camera.) If you purchase a tripod that's not rated for the weight of your camera, it won't be stable enough to ensure that you get sharp pictures. Make sure to note the weight of the camera with your heaviest lens and external flash attached.

Figure 1-8: *A tripod steadies the camera during a lengthy exposure.*

> **TIP**
>
> Purchase a case that is water repellent that you can use to protect your camera in inclement weather. Another useful feature is an internal waterproof pocket for storing memory cards.

> **TIP**
>
> If you shop for a tripod online, make sure you visit the tripod manufacturer's website for detailed specifications.

Decide which accessories you'd like on your tripod. A spirit level is a nice accessory as it enables you to adjust the tripod so that the camera is perfectly level. A tripod case is another handy accessory.

Choose an External Flash

Many high-end digital cameras and all digital SLR cameras come with a hot shoe that enables you to attach an external flash to the camera. External flash units are more powerful than the ones built into digital cameras, and they present you with wonderful options such as bounce lighting. Figure 1-9 shows an external flash unit for a Canon EOS 10D or Digital Rebel camera.

*Figure 1-9: **External flash units are more powerful than built-in camera flash units.***

Add an External Storage Device

If you travel frequently and shoot lots of pictures during your trips, you'll need to invest in a lot of memory cards, carry a laptop computer with you, or purchase an external storage device (Figure 1-10). External storage devices are battery powered. You use them to copy the images from memory cards to the storage device, which is usually a hard drive. There are also external storage devices that you can use to copy your images to a CD or DVD. After you download the images to the portable storage device, format the memory card and continue shooting. If you own two memory cards, you can use one to continue shooting pictures while the portable storage device is downloading your other memory card. After you return from your trip, connect the pocket drive to your computer and download the images.

If you purchase an external flash manufactured by a third party, make sure it's compatible with your digital camera. Otherwise, you run the risk of damaging your camera's circuitry.

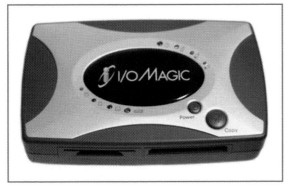

*Figure 1-10: **You can store digital photos on a pocket hard drive.***

1
2
3
4
5
6
7
8
9
10

Purchase a Photo-Quality Printer

The popularity of digital photography has spawned a plethora of photo-quality printers. This is another case where it pays to do a bit of research and shopping before buying. Low-priced photo-quality printers are available with three-color inks and black, but the better models have six-color inks and black. Many photo-quality printers also have built-in card readers that enable you to print images from your memory card without needing a computer, as shown in Figure 1-11. Visit a store that carries the printer you are interested in. Bring a memory card that holds some colorful photos you have taken, and ask the salesperson if you can test the printer by creating a couple of 4 × 6 prints of your images.

*Figure 1-11: **You can print images directly from your camera with some printers.***

How To...

Chapter 2

Getting the Most from Your Camera

Digital cameras have different controls and settings than conventional film cameras. Many of the controls and settings are included in the camera's menu. While each camera is somewhat different, they do share similar controls and settings. Point-and-shoot digital cameras are the easiest to operate, while high-end digital SLR cameras have more settings and controls. In this chapter, you'll learn the basics of how to take pictures with a digital camera.

Record Images with Your Digital Camera

Digital photography is all about instant gratification. No matter what type of digital camera you own, you don't have to wait for prints to be processed before you know whether or not you got the shot. A second or so after you take the

Camera mode dial

Figure 2-1: A point-and-shoot digital camera has a dial to select the desired shooting mode.

NOTE

If your camera does not have a through-the-lens viewfinder, composing through the viewfinder may produce undesirable results, such as your subject being in the wrong part of the picture. If you're taking a portrait or zooming in tight on your subject, compose your picture through the LCD viewer to achieve the desired composition.

picture, it appears on the camera's LCD monitor. If you don't like what you see, delete it. The following sections show you the basics of how to record an image with the different types of digital cameras on the market. You'll also learn specific techniques to get the maximum from your digital camera in the latter parts of this chapter.

Use a Point-and-Shoot Digital Camera

When you use a point-and-shoot camera, the camera takes care of pretty much everything for you, with the exception of choosing the subject and composing the picture. However, even the simplest point-and-shoot camera is equipped with different shooting modes (as shown in Figure 2-1) to compensate for backlit subjects, fast-moving subjects, and so on.

1. Turn the camera mode dial to select the desired shooting mode.
2. Compose your picture through the viewfinder or LCD viewer. If desired, use your camera zoom control to zoom in on your subject and achieve the perfect composition.
3. Press the shutter halfway to focus on your center of interest. Most cameras will flash a green dot to signify that focus has been achieved. You may also hear a beep.
4. Press the shutter to take the picture. After you take the picture, you may see an hourglass or some other symbol that signifies that the camera is processing the picture. A few seconds later, the processed picture appears in the LCD viewer.

Shoot Pictures with a High-End Digital Camera

If you own a high-end digital camera, you can exercise creative control over your pictures. In addition to having shooting modes to compensate for lighting conditions and fast moving objects, you also have an aperture priority shooting mode, shutter priority shooting mode, and manual shooting mode. Many high-end cameras feature a wide range of focal lengths and enable you to view the image through an electronic viewfinder that shows you exactly what will be recorded by the camera image sensor. These cameras are also referred to as

Figure 2-2: A high-end camera has more features and creative shooting modes.

Zoom Lens Reflex digital cameras. Figure 2-2 shows a high-end digital camera that features an electronic viewfinder and focal lengths that range from 28mm to 280mm (35mm equivalent).

1. Turn the camera mode dial to the desired shooting mode. If you choose one of the preset modes, go to step 4.

2. If desired, select the metering mode. Most high-end digital cameras have three metering modes: evaluative (also known as matrix or multi-pattern) metering, partial metering, and center-weighted (also known as spot) metering. You'll learn how to select the proper metering mode for the conditions under which you are shooting in the section "Choose the Proper Metering Mode."

3. If you choose a creative mode, you'll have to adjust the shutter speed when shooting in shutter priority mode or aperture when shooting in aperture priority mode. If you're shooting in manual mode, you adjust the shutter speed and aperture to achieve the desired exposure.

4. Compose your scene through the viewfinder or LCD viewer. Most high-end cameras feature a through-the-lens viewfinder, which allows you to accurately compose the scene based on what the image sensor is recording. Some photographers prefer to compose their pictures using the LCD monitor.

5. Press the shutter button halfway to achieve focus. The camera gives you a visual warning in the viewfinder or LCD monitor when focus has been achieved. A beep may also sound depending on the model of the camera.

6. Press the shutter button fully to take the picture. Modern high-end cameras respond quickly. You'll soon see the processed image in the LCD viewer.

Shoot Images with a Digital SLR

When you shoot images with a digital SLR, you have the utmost in creative freedom. You can capture images with a wide array of lenses—everything from a super wide-angle fish-eye lens, to a long telephoto lens with a focal length of 500mm or greater. You can use a wide-angle lens to record a picturesque landscape and then quickly change to a telephoto to capture a close-up of a distant animal. Figure 2-3 shows a digital SLR with additional lenses.

Figure 2-3: You have complete creative control when you shoot images with a digital SLR.

1. Select the proper lens for the scene you are going to capture and swap it with the current lens.

CAUTION

When you change lenses, you run the risk of getting dust on the CMOS image sensor because the current to the CMOS can act as a dust magnet. Dust on the sensor will show up as specks on your image. You can reduce the risk of getting dust on the CMOS if you turn off the camera power prior to changing lenses.

TIP

If the camera is unable to achieve focus in low light conditions, momentarily shine a penlight on the area you want the camera to focus on. After focus has been achieved, turn off the penlight and take the picture. Alternatively, you can switch to manual focus.

TIP

For images you're going to e-mail, you can get by with an image size as low as 640 x 480 pixels. Choose normal image quality mode.

2. Turn the camera mode dial to select the desired shooting mode. If you choose one of the creative modes, you'll need to adjust the shutter speed, aperture, or both.

3. Choose the proper metering mode for the scene. Metering modes will be covered in detail in the "Choose the Proper Metering Mode" section.

4. Compose the scene through the camera viewfinder. With a digital SLR, you're looking right through the lens, so what you see is what you get.

5. Press the shutter button halfway to achieve focus. The camera will flash a visual warning in the viewfinder when focus has been achieved. Your camera may also beep when focus is achieved.

6. Press the shutter button fully to take the picture. Soon you'll see the image on the camera's LCD viewer.

Utilize All of Your Camera's Features

Whether you own the simplest point-and-shoot digital camera, a sophisticated high-end digital camera, or a digital SLR, you'll get better pictures if you learn to utilize all of your camera's features. Your camera has controls that you can use to gain control of the picture-taking process, for example in difficult lighting conditions, such as photographing a person on a brightly lit beach. Your camera also has controls that determine image size and quality.

Set Image Size and Quality

1. Power up your camera.

2. Press the menu button.

3. Navigate to the menu item that determines image size and quality.

4. Select the desired image size and quality. Figure 2-4 shows the image size and quality menu for a Canon EOS10D.

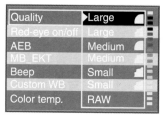

Quality	Large
Red-eye on/off	Large
AEB	Medium
MB_EKT	Medium
Beep	Small
Custom WB	Small
Color temp.	RAW

Figure 2-4: Setting the image size and quality.

QUICKSTEPS

SAVING THE MAXIMUM NUMBER OF IMAGES TO YOUR MEMORY CARD

The file size of an image is determined by the image size and quality you specify. If you own a high megapixel camera and shoot at the largest image size and best quality, your image file sizes will be quite large. If you don't have spare memory cards or a device to download the images to, your memory card may run out of room. You can conserve space on your memory card by choosing a smaller image size and lower quality for the images you'll share via e-mail because they don't need the same high resolution as images you'll print. You can also gain additional space on a memory card by deleting unwanted images. However, this does sap battery power. Some digital cameras are notoriously hard on batteries, so delete images with caution. Delete unwanted images only if you have a spare battery on hand, or you have plenty of power left in the camera battery.

CONSERVING YOUR MEMORY CARD

1. Monitor the number of images you'll be able to save to your memory card. Many cameras display the number of images captured and remaining number of images that can be saved to the card. Refer to your camera manual for further information.

2. Press the camera menu button.

3. Navigate to the image size and quality section of your menu.

4. Choose a smaller image size and quality.

Match the Metering Mode to Conditions

If you own a high-end digital camera or a digital SLR, you can choose the metering mode that best suits the conditions under which you are shooting the picture. The subject matter also plays a part in the metering mode you choose. Camera manufacturers refer to metering modes by different names. The most common designations and their descriptions are listed in the following table. You can choose from these metering modes:

METERING MODE	DESCRIPTION	METERING MODE ICON
Evaluative, matrix, or multi-pattern	Multi-pattern metering (also called evaluative or matrix metering) is a good choice for many shots and may be suitable for backlit subjects if the light source does not put the subject in heavy shade. The scene is metered from multiple metering zones, which are linked and averaged to determine the exposure for the scene.	◉
Center-weighted average	Use this mode when the background is significantly brighter than the subject. The scene is metered from a small area around the center of the scene.	
Partial or spot	Use this mode when your subject is in the center of the scene. The metering is weighted toward the center of the scene and averaged for the entire scene.	○

Choose the Proper Metering Mode

1. Analyze the scene through the viewfinder. If the scene has even lighting, you should use evaluative (some camera manufacturers refer to this mode as matrix or multi-pattern) metering. If you're photographing a person or subject in front of a bright light source such as the sun, you should use center-weighted average metering mode. If your subject is the most important part of the scene, use partial (some camera manufacturers refer to this mode as spot) metering and make sure you aim the metering mode icon in the center of your camera viewfinder at your subject.

2. Press the button or make the menu choice for the desired metering mode. Refer to your camera manual for detailed information on changing metering modes.

3. Compose the picture.

4. Press the shutter button halfway to focus the scene.

5. Press the shutter button fully to take the picture.

Lock Exposure

When you compose a photograph, you have a center of interest. This is the point of the photograph to which you want to draw the viewer's attention. Inexperienced photographers have a bad habit of placing the subject in the center of a scene, which can often lead to a boring photograph. Photographers often compose a picture where the center of interest is off center. If you compose pictures where your main subject is not centered in the viewfinder, you'll have to lock focus on the off-center subject using the auto-focus point and then compose the picture. Many cameras provide a method for locking exposure to the auto-focus point.

Shoot an Off-Center Subject

1. Position the camera so that the subject is in the center of the viewfinder.

2. Push the shutter button halfway to lock focus and exposure.

3. Continue to hold the shutter button halfway and compose the scene.

4. Press the shutter button fully to record the image.

NOTE

Some cameras require you to push a button to lock exposure. Refer to your camera manual for additional information on locking exposure.

Focus the Scene

When you press the shutter button halfway, your camera focuses on a subject in your scene based on the metering mode you choose. When you choose evaluative (or matrix or multi-pattern) metering mode, the camera has several auto-focus points and will focus on the closest object in the scene that intersects with an auto-focus point. When you use the center-weighted average or partial (also called spot) metering mode, the camera focuses on the closest object in the middle of the scene. High-end digital cameras and digital SLR cameras usually have two auto-focus modes: a one-shot mode for still subjects and a mode where the camera focuses continuously on a moving subject.

Select Auto-Focus Mode

1. Press your camera focus mode button.
2. Choose the desired auto-focus mode. Alternatively, you may need to use the camera menu to change focus modes. Refer to your camera manual for detailed instructions.
3. Compose and shoot the picture.

Focus on an Off-Center Subject

1. Select center-weighted average or partial (or spot) metering mode.
2. Position your camera so that the subject you want in focus is in the center of the viewfinder.
3. Press the shutter button halfway to achieve focus.
4. Compose the scene with the shutter button still pressed halfway.
5. Press the shutter button fully to record the picture.

TIP

Your camera may also have a mode that switches between one-shot focus and continuous focus depending on the subject matter you are shooting.

Use Preset Shooting Modes

When you shoot a picture using your camera's automatic mode, the camera exposes the picture based on the scene lighting, the objects in the scene, and the scene colors. This mode works well for average conditions. However, when you're shooting pictures in adverse lighting conditions or shooting pictures of fast moving objects, you'll have to switch to one of your camera's preset modes. The following table lists the shooting modes you're likely to find on your camera mode dial.

SHOOTING MODE	DESCRIPTION	ICON
Close-up	Enables you to shoot close-ups of subjects like flowers and butterflies.	
Portrait	Blurs the background to make the subject of your portrait the center of attention.	
Landscape	Used for scenic shots. The camera chooses a lens aperture that keeps near and distant objects in focus.	
Sports	Selects a high shutter speed to freeze fast moving objects. The camera continually focuses on the moving object.	
Night portrait	Uses the flash to illuminate your subject and leaves the shutter open to record the ambient scenery. You should mount your camera on a tripod when using this mode as the slow shutter speed may cause blurring. Your subject should remain perfectly still during the exposure.	
Flash off	Prevents the flash from firing. In this mode, your camera will adjust the exposure to take the picture using the ambient scene lighting. Note that this may result in long exposures, which will require you to mount the camera on a tripod to ensure a razor-sharp image.	

NOTE

Some cameras have a button to turn off camera flash.

(a)

(b)

(c)

Figure 2-6: An image shot with minimum settings for sharpness, contrast, and saturation (a). An image shot with default settings for sharpness, contrast, and saturation (b). An image shot with maximum settings for sharpness, contrast, and saturation (c).

Select a Shooting Mode

1. Analyze the scene to determine if you need to switch from automatic mode.

2. Select the desired shooting mode from your camera shoot mode dial. Figure 2-5 shows the shooting mode dial for a Canon S1 IS.

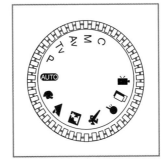

Figure 2-5: Select the proper shooting mode.

3. Compose and shoot the picture.

Enhance Images with Camera Controls

Many digital cameras are equipped with menu options that enable you to enhance images. If your camera is so equipped, you can change image sharpness, contrast, and saturation. Consult your owner's manual to see which menu command is used to set each of these. Figure 2-6a shows an image shot with the sharpness, contrast, and saturation set to their minimum values; Figure 2-6b shows an image shot with default settings for sharpness, contrast, and saturation; and Figure 2-6c shows an image shot with maximum settings for sharpness, contrast, and saturation.

Shoot Images Using Creative Shooting Modes

High-end digital cameras and digital SLR cameras give you the option of shooting images using "creative" shooting modes. When you shoot using one of the creative shooting modes (aperture priority, shutter priority, and with some cameras, program mode), you use the camera controls to create the desired image. When you shoot in aperture priority mode, you set the f-stop, which determines how much of the image is in focus (depth of field). When you shoot in shutter priority mode you choose the desired shutter speed to freeze action, or creatively blur the image. When you shoot in aperture priority mode, you select the desired aperture and the camera sets the shutter speed; in shutter priority mode, you select the desired shutter speed and the camera sets the aperture.

Capture Images Using Aperture Priority Mode

1. Turn the camera mode dial to the aperture priority icon. Many cameras use the abbreviation Av for aperture priority mode.

2. Choose the desired f-stop. Refer to your camera manual for the control that sets the f-stop.

3. Compose and shoot the picture.

Understand Lens f-Stops

The aperture setting is known as the f-stop. The lowest number f-stop lets the most amount of light reach the image sensor. The next f-stop lets half as much light reach the sensor and so on. You control depth of field with f-stops. When you choose a low f-stop such as f/2.8, more light reaches the image sensor and the depth of field is limited; objects behind your subject and in the foreground are blurry, as shown in Figure 2-7. A low f-stop is ideal for portraits. Notice how your attention is drawn to the model while the background is a colorful blur. When you choose a high f-stop number such as f/16, less light reaches the image sensor and more of your image is in focus, which is desirable when

Figure 2-7: *A low f-stop provides a limited depth of field.*

Figure 2-8: *A high f-stop increases the depth of field.*

you're shooting a landscape, as shown in Figure 2-8. Notice how the entire image is sharp, from the tiny blades of grass in the sand to the art deco hotel in the distance.

Capture Images Using Shutter Priority Mode

1. Turn the camera mode dial to the shutter priority icon. Many cameras use the abbreviation Tv for shutter priority mode.

2. Choose the desired shutter speed. Refer to your camera manual for the control that sets the shutter speed.

3. Compose and shoot the picture.

Understand Shutter Speeds

The shutter speed determines how long the shutter remains open to record the scene. Shutter speeds are measured in fractions of a second or, when shooting a long exposure, in seconds. If you're shooting in dim conditions without a flash, you'll need a slow shutter speed such as 1/15 second. The rule of thumb for the slowest shutter speed at which you can handhold a camera is the reciprocal of the lens focal length. In other words, if you're shooting an image with a digital SLR using a 20mm lens, you'll need a tripod with any shutter speed slower than 1/20 second. You can, however, use a slow shutter speed to create artistic blurs such as the headlight patterns shown in Figure 2-9. Slow shutter speeds are also useful when photographing a stationary subject in dim lighting conditions. If you're photographing a subject with a slow shutter speed, your subject must remain perfectly still; otherwise, the image will be blurred. When you shoot at a high shutter

Figure 2-9: *You use a slow shutter speed to record images in dim lighting without a flash.*

speed such as 1/2000 second, you freeze action, as shown in Figure 2-10. To avoid blurry images when you're using a high-end digital camera with a zoom lens, you'll need to shoot with a faster shutter speed when you zoom in tight on a subject. When in doubt, a tripod will always ensure that the camera remains steady while you're taking the picture.

Figure 2-10: *You use a high shutter speed to freeze action.*

QUICKSTEPS

DEALING WITH DIGITAL NOISE

If you capture pictures using ISO settings higher than ISO 400, you may notice digital noise in the form of colored specks in the picture. Digital noise is most noticeable when images are magnified. Cameras with high ISO ratings usually have a noise filter you can access via a menu command. Refer to your camera manual to see if your camera has this feature.

REDUCING DIGITAL NOISE

1. Select the desired ISO setting from your camera menu.
2. Select the noise filter option from your camera menu.
3. Compose and shoot the picture.

Choose the ISO Setting

With a traditional film camera, you choose the film speed to match the conditions under which you'll be shooting: you use low-speed film in bright light, or high-speed film in dim light. High-end digital cameras and digital SLR cameras enable you to choose the ISO setting to suit the scene you are recording, which is like changing film speed on the fly. For example, if you're inside a museum that prohibits flash photography, you can choose a higher ISO setting that enables you to shoot at a higher shutter speed to avoid camera blur. ISO settings for digital cameras range from ISO 50 to ISO 3200. Consult your camera manual for the ISO range available for your camera.

NOTE

After you finish shooting pictures in low light with a high ISO setting, remember to choose a lower setting when you shoot pictures in well-lit locations.

TIP

If your camera doesn't have a digital noise filter, mount your camera on a tripod and shoot several pictures in low light without a flash. Shoot the first picture at the lowest ISO setting, the second picture at the next highest ISO setting, and so on. Download the pictures to your computer and preview them to see the ISO setting at which digital noise becomes visible.

Increase Camera Sensitivity

1. Press your camera's menu button. Alternatively, certain cameras have a button devoted to accessing camera functions or adjusting the ISO setting.

2. Select the desired ISO setting.

3. Compose and shoot the picture.

Zoom in on Your Subject

Every digital camera features a zoom lens of some sort. Point-and-shoot digital cameras generally feature an optical zoom with a maximum magnification of 2X or 3X, while high-end digital cameras may have a zoom with a magnification as high as 10X. Your camera may also have digital zoom. Images captured with digital zoom are coarser than images captured with optical zoom. Figure 2-11 shows an image of an antique camera captured with optical zoom, and

*Figure 2-11: **Optical zoom enemies you to get close to subjects.***

*Figure 2-11: **Optical zoom enables you to get close to subjects.***

Figure 2-12 shows an image of the lens of the same antique camera captured with digital zoom. Notice that the close-up shot with digital zoom is not as sharp as the image shot with optical zoom. The difference in detail becomes more apparent if the image is printed on a high-resolution inkjet or dye-sublimation printer.

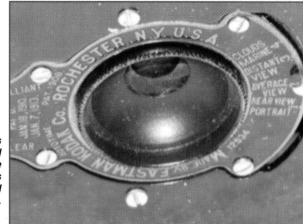

Figure 2-12: Images captured with digital zoom don't have the detail of images captured with optical zoom.

TIP

Many cameras with high degrees of optical zoom have some sort of image stabilization feature. Use image stabilization when you are zooming in tight on a subject to prevent blur from camera movement. You should also use a higher shutter speed when zooming to maximum magnification.

NOTE

Some cameras have a menu option to enable digital zoom. Refer to your camera manual for additional information.

Use Optical Zoom

1. Point the camera toward the subject.
2. Press the zoom button to zoom in on the subject.
3. Compose and shoot the picture.

Use Digital Zoom

1. Point your camera toward the subject.
2. Press the zoom button until maximum optical zoom has been achieved.
3. Continue to press the zoom button to activate digital zoom.
4. Zoom in to the desired magnification.
5. Compose and shoot the picture.

Cope with Lighting Conditions

When objects are viewed in different lighting conditions, the three primary colors (red, green, and blue) exist in varying proportions depending on the color temperature of the light source. As the color temperature changes, the color cast changes. When a color temperature is high, there is more blue. When the color temperature is low, there is more red. The human eye compensates for color temperature. When you view a white object under a fluorescent light, it appears white. However, the same object has a greenish cast when recorded by a camera image sensor. Your camera probably has AWB (Automatic White Balance), which compensates for color temperature under most conditions. However, if you notice that your images have a color cast, as shown in Figure 2-13a, you'll have to manually set the white balance using your camera menu settings. Figure 2-13b shows the same subject with the white balance adjusted properly.

(a)

(b)

Figure 2-13: If your images exhibit a color cast, you'll need to adjust the white balance (a). The same subject after the white balance has been properly adjusted (b).

Some cameras have external buttons to adjust white balance. Refer to your camera manual for detailed instructions on setting white balance for your model camera.

Many high-end cameras give you the option to create a custom white balance setting by photographing a white piece of paper and then using a menu command to calibrate the camera white balance to the image you just photographed. Refer to your camera manual for additional details.

Set White Balance

1. Access your camera menu.
2. Choose the white balance setting to suit your scene. The following table shows the most commonly used icons for white balance settings, the corresponding lighting condition, and the color temperature.

WHITE BALANCE ICON	LIGHTING CONDITION	COLOR TEMPERATURE
☀	Outdoors, sunny daylight	5200 Kelvin
🏠	Outdoors, shade	7000 Kelvin
☁	Cloudy, hazy conditions and sunsets	6000 Kelvin
☀	Tungsten (light bulb) light	3200 Kelvin
☼	Fluorescent light	4000 Kelvin
⚡	Camera flash	6000 Kelvin

Get the Most from Your Digital Camera

After you gain experience in photography, you'll probably branch out and use your camera more creatively. For example, when taking portraits, you'll rotate the camera 90 degrees to capture a head and shoulders portrait or head shot. Your camera may have an option to auto-rotate images taken in portrait format 90 degrees. Your camera may also have the option to record movies. The size and frame rate of movies varies depends on the camera model. Most digital cameras record movies with a frame size of 320 × 240 pixels and a frame rate of 15fps (frames per second). You can use short movies in this format for e-mail attachments, or for viewing on websites. If you have a high-end digital camera, you may be able to record movies with a larger frame size and higher frame rate that you can save to a CD.

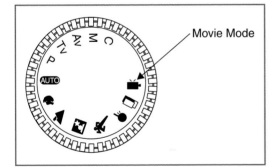

*Figure 2-14: **You can shoot movies with many digital cameras.***

Auto-Rotate Images

1. Access your camera menu.
2. Navigate to the auto-rotate feature.
3. Enable the option.

Shoot Movies with Your Digital Camera

1. Turn your camera mode dial to the movie icon.
   Figure 2-14 shows the camera mode dial for a Canon S1 IS.
2. If applicable, select the frame size and frame rate. Refer to your camera manual for detailed information on these settings.

MAXIMIZING CAMERA BATTERY LIFE

As you gain experience with your digital camera, you'll use it more often and shoot more pictures in a single setting. Battery life varies depending on the model of the camera you own and the number of features you use. When you power up the camera, an icon appears that indicates the state of the battery charge. Most cameras issue some kind of warning when you're about to exhaust the battery. There's nothing more frustrating than running out of battery when you're photographing beautiful scenery. If your camera uses alkaline batteries, carry a spare set with you. If your camera uses a rechargeable lithium ion battery, purchase an extra battery and keep the fully charged spare in your camera bag. Another option you may want to consider is a battery charger that works off a car cigarette lighter. That way you can recharge an exhausted battery and shoot pictures with your spare. You can also change certain menu settings and do other things to maximize the life of your battery.

CONSERVING THE CAMERA BATTERY

1. Access your camera menu and change the following settings:

   - Set the image review to the shortest interval. This determines the amount of time an image is displayed after you take a picture. Shorter review times conserve battery power.

   - Set the power saving mode to the shortest interval. This determines the amount of time before the camera goes into sleep mode, which conserves battery power.

2. Whenever possible, use the camera viewfinder to compose your scene as the LCD viewer uses more power.

Continued . . .

3. Press the record button to begin recording your movie.

4. Press the record button to finish recording your movie.

Maintain Your Digital Camera

Digital cameras are more complex and more expensive than their film-dependent brethren. You can lengthen the life of your equipment and ensure that the camera remains in peak operating condition if you follow a few simple steps.

Maintain Your Equipment

1. Clean the camera body with a soft cloth or microfiber cloth. Never use any solvents on the camera body.

2. Clean the camera viewfinder with a blower brush to remove dust and debris. Then wipe the viewfinder clean with a microfiber cloth.

3. Clean the camera lens with a blower brush to remove loose dust and debris. Gently wipe the lens with a microfiber cloth. If you own a digital SLR, remember to clean the rear element of each lens you own as well as the front element. Many camera stores sell digital camera cleaning kits like the one shown in Figure 2-15.

*Figure 2-15: **You can purchase an inexpensive cleaning kit from your local camera store.***

3. Don't erase an image unless absolutely necessary. Erasing images consumes battery power.

4. Use camera zoom sparingly. The motor to power the camera zoom uses battery power.

5. Only use the camera flash when necessary. If you get in the habit of shooting with natural light, you'll conserve battery power and get more natural looking pictures to boot.

6. When shooting in cold climates, keep your camera warm when not in use. One method is to store the camera between your body and coat.

Battery life is shorter when you're shooting in a cold climate. Keep your spare battery in your pocket to keep it warm. If you're not going to use your camera for a few weeks, remove the battery to prevent trickle discharge.

TIP

When traveling in a car, always secure your camera. If you have to brake suddenly, and the camera is not secure, it will continue moving at the speed of the car until it strikes something solid like the dashboard, which can severely damage the sensitive circuitry in your camera. If you're traveling alone, place your camera bag in the passenger's seat and secure it with the seatbelt. If you own a point-and-shoot camera that you house in a small case, keep the camera in your glove box, or some other location in the car where it won't become airborne if you have to suddenly brake.

Clean a Digital SLR Image Sensor

If you own a digital SLR and notice what looks like dust specks on your images, you may need to clean your camera's CMOS or CCD. You clean the camera image sensor by removing the lens and then using a menu command to flip up the mirror. While the mirror is locked in the upward position, use a gentle burst of air from a blower brush to dislodge any dust that may have accumulated on the image sensor when you changed lenses. Do not touch the image sensor with the blower brush. *Never* use a compressed air canister to clean the image sensor because compressed air canisters contain liquid propellants that will be blown onto the image sensor. If you foul the image sensor with a liquid, you'll have to take your camera to a camera store to professionally clean the image sensor. Refer to your camera manual for detailed instructions on cleaning your camera image sensor.

If you own a digital SLR, consider purchasing a skylight filter for each lens you own. The filters are relatively inexpensive and will protect the front lens element from damage. The skylight filter screws into the front of the lens as shown in this illustration:

Chapter 3
Shooting Like a Pro

Anybody can take a photograph by pointing a camera at something and pressing the shutter button. However, to take a good photograph requires a bit of skill, thought, and creativity. There are several time-honored rules for taking photographs. In this chapter, you'll learn some of these rules, as well as other techniques for taking pictures like a pro.

Take Pictures Like a Pro

When you become proficient with your camera and its controls, you'll be ready to take your photography to the next level. You can create compelling photographs suitable for framing with your digital camera. In this chapter, you'll learn several techniques for taking professional-quality images.

Compose the Photograph

1. Preview the scene through your viewfinder or LCD monitor.

2. Be aware of any obvious problems like garbage cans in the background. Also be on the lookout for trees or telephone poles that appear to be growing out of your subject's head.

3. Imagine a grid of nine squares over your scene and place your center of interest where two gridlines intersect. This is known as the Rule of Thirds. The image in Figure 3-1 was composed with the waterfall as the center of interest.

4. Focus on your center of interest. For more information on focusing, see Chapter 2.

5. Shoot the picture.

Figure 3-1: Place your center of interest according to the Rule of Thirds.

TIP

Every rule is made to be broken. Before you take a photograph, examine the scene from several vantage points to determine the best composition. In most instances the Rule of Thirds is the way to go, but other images are better when shot from straight on.

TIP

You can also use parts of the scene to compose the photograph. For example, a curving path or walkway is an ideal element to draw a viewer into the scene, as shown in the following illustration.

QUICKSTEPS

MATCHING YOUR COMPOSITION TO THE SCENE

Beginning photographers rarely think of rotating the camera. However, if your subject is vertical, rotating the camera 90 degrees will give you a more interesting composition. For example, if you're photographing a tall waterfall, rotating the camera 90 degrees guarantees you a more interesting image.

ROTATE THE CAMERA

1. Analyze the objects in your scene.

2. Rotate the camera 90 degrees if your subject is vertical. The following image shows Bridal Veil Falls in Yosemite National Park as photographed with the camera rotated 90 degrees.

Use Selective Focus

Another important decision you make when taking a photograph is how much of the scene will be in focus. If you're photographing a landscape, you want everything in the scene to be in focus; when photographing a person or group of people, you don't want the background to distract from the subject matter. If you have a camera capable of capturing images in aperture priority mode, you determine how much of the scene is in apparent focus by choosing the proper f-stop.

Determine the Depth of Field

1. Switch to aperture priority shooting mode.

2. Analyze the scene through your camera viewfinder or LCD viewer.

3. Rotate your camera's control that sets the f-stop. Select an f-stop of f /11 or higher (small aperture) when photographing a landscape, as shown in Figure 3-2. Select the lowest f-stop number (large aperture) when photographing a person, as shown in Figure 3-3.

Figure 3-2: Use a small aperture to photograph a landscape.

*Figure 3-3: **Use a large aperture to capture a portrait.***

4. If you're using a point-and-shoot camera that doesn't have an aperture priority mode, switch to Landscape mode to maintain a large depth of field, or Portrait mode to maintain a shallow depth of field where only your main subject is in focus.

Avoid Lens Distortion

A zoom lens is a wonderful thing. It gives you the creative freedom to compose a scene as you see fit. However, when not used properly, a zoom lens can ruin an otherwise pleasing image. For example, when photographing a building, beginning photographers have a tendency to get as close as possible and then zoom out to get the entire building into the frame. This can lead to distortion because parallel lines will appear to converge, as shown in Figure 3-4. To avoid distortion, it's best to back away from the building and then zoom *in* to get the desired composition, as shown in Figure 3-5.

*Figure 3-4: **Images will be distorted if you use the wrong focal length.***

*Figure 3-5: **Move away from the scene and zoom in to capture an image with no distortion.***

NOTE

If you angle the camera to capture an image of a tall building, your image will be distorted as the lines at the top of the picture will converge. This distortion can be desirable for artistic images. However, if you want a true rendition of the scene, back up until the entire building is visible in the viewfinder.

Choose the Right Focal Length

1. Examine the scene through the viewfinder or LCD monitor.
2. As you preview the scene, pay attention to vertical lines. If they appear to be converging at the top of the viewfinder, back away from the scene.
3. Zoom in to achieve the desired composition.
4. Shoot the picture.

Get a Perfect Exposure Every Time

If you own a high-end digital camera, chances are you have options to bracket the exposure. Professional photographers bracket an exposure to make sure they'll get the shot. When an exposure is bracketed, three pictures are taken: one with the exposure determined by the camera as shown in Figure 3-6b, one that is underexposed as shown in Figure 3-6a, and one that is overexposed as shown in Figure 3-6c. When you set up auto-exposure bracketing, you determine the

(a)   *(b)*   *(c)*

Figure 3-6: The image underexposed by one f-stop (a); the image with the camera-recommended exposure (b); and the image overexposed by one f-stop (c).

amount the images are underexposed and overexposed. Typical settings let you vary from half an f-stop to two f-stops. Auto-exposure bracketing ensures that one of the images will be properly exposed. When you download the images to your computer, you can save the image that suits your needs and discard the others.

Hedge Your Bets with Auto-Exposure Bracketing

1. Access your camera menu.

2. Choose the **Auto-Exposure Bracketing** option. Figure 3-7 shows the auto-exposure bracketing menu for a Canon EOS-10D.

3. Set the amount you want the bracketed images to be underexposed and overexposed. Refer to your camera manual for detailed instructions.

4. Close the camera menu and shoot the desired images.

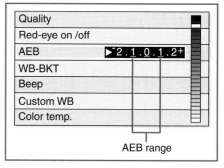

Quality	
Red-eye on /off	
AEB	▶2.1.0.1.2+
WB-BKT	
Beep	
Custom WB	
Color temp.	

AEB range

*Figure 3-7: **You set the auto-exposure bracketing amount with your camera menu.***

NOTE

With some camera models, you may have to enable the continuous drive option, which enables you to take multiple pictures while the shutter button is pressed.

Capture Images in Perfect Light

If you've ever looked at a photograph and been taken in by its beauty, you'll probably notice it has very warm tones. Those warm tones are best captured when you photograph your images in the morning or late afternoon. During the middle of the day, the sun shines down from overhead. The light is direct and harsh and doesn't cast flattering shadows. Unless you have a reason for including the sun in the picture, shoot with your back to the sun and try to avoid getting your shadow in the picture.

Figure 3-8: Images photographed in the morning have warm tones.

Shoot Images at the Right Time of Day

1. Shoot images in morning light to get images like Figure 3-8.

2. Shoot images in the late afternoon to get images similar to Figure 3-9.

Figure 3-9: Late afternoon sun is also ideal for taking pictures.

Take Advantage of Atmospheric Conditions

You can also get wonderful pictures when you might think you'd be better off leaving your camera at home. That is, you can take advantage of the soft diffuse light when it's foggy, misty, or overcast to capture some interesting images, although you'll have to shoot a higher ISO rating because of the low light. If your camera is capable of shooting close-ups, photograph flowers in the early morning. The dewdrops add compelling highlights to your pictures. If you get a bit of digital noise, it will add to the effect. Just make sure to protect your digital camera when photographing in inclement conditions.

QUICKSTEPS

CREATING FOG

If you're faced with harsh conditions and the lighting isn't perfect, you can quickly transform conditions by creating fog. If the air is humid enough, simply blow a few breaths onto the glass portion of the camera lens. Wait a second or two for the mist to dissipate, and then take your picture. This technique works with all digital cameras. However, you'll be able to judge exactly how fogged over your lens is if you own a digital SLR, or a Zoom Lens Reflex digital camera that has a through-the-lens viewfinder. If you own a simple point-and-shoot digital camera, breathe on the lens and watch the LCD monitor to determine how misted over the lens is. The following shows an image taken using this technique.

Create Dreamy Images

1. Shoot images in cloudy and overcast conditions to capture images like the one in Figure 3-10.

Figure 3-10: Cloudy, overcast conditions produce soft diffuse lighting.

2. Shoot close-ups of flowers in the early morning to capture images like the one in Figure 3-11. Notice the flower was also photographed with a large lens aperture (a small f-stop number such as 2.8), so that the background is out of focus.

Figure 3-11: Dewdrops add wonderful highlights to close-ups of flowers.

Flash Photography

When you're shooting in total darkness or dimly lit rooms, you have no other choice but to enable your camera flash. When you photograph with a flash, you often wash out a picture because of the harshness of the flash. You can correct this to some extent by editing the image in an image-editing application. You can also use your camera flash to fill in shadows. For example, if you're photographing someone in a shaded area with their back to the sun, or if your subject is wearing a large hat, fill flash can be used to lighten the shaded areas.

Use Camera Flash

1. Set your camera shooting mode dial to automatic.
2. Press the shutter button halfway. The on-camera flash will pop up in low lighting conditions.
3. Compose and shoot the picture.

Use Fill Flash

1. Switch to one of the creative shooting modes.
2. Press your camera flash button to pop up the flash. Most camera flash buttons look like a lightning bolt.
3. Push the shutter button halfway to establish focus. The camera flash will fire a test shot to determine how much light is needed.
4. Press the shutter button fully to take the picture. Figure 3-12 shows an image photographed with fill flash.

*Figure 3-12: **You can use fill flash to photograph a shaded subject.***

TIP

In low lighting conditions, your camera may have a hard time establishing focus. Aiming a small penlight at your center of interest will help the camera establish focus on that part of the scene.

PHOTOGRAPHING PEOPLE WITH FLASH

When you photograph a person, pet, or group of people with a flash camera, you may see a condition known as red-eye. This occurs because the subject's pupils are dilated to cope with the dim light. The camera flash bounces off the person's retina back into the camera and makes a person's eyes look red and pets' eyes look white. If your camera has a red-eye reduction feature, the camera fires a preflash, which causes the subject's pupil to close down and avoid the dilation that causes the red-eye.

DEALING WITH RED-EYE

1. Access your camera menu.

2. Enable red-eye reduction. Refer to your camera manual for the location of your red-eye reduction menu command.

3. Tell the subject to look at the red-eye reduction lamp. Refer to your camera manual for the exact location of this device on your camera.

4. Compose and shoot the picture.

TIP

The red-eye reduction preflash may also cause the subject to blink, which means your subject's eyes may be closed when the main flash goes off. You'll get a more natural picture if you correct the red-eye in an image-editing program such as Adobe Photoshop Elements.

Use Advanced Flash Options

If you own a high-end digital camera or a digital SLR camera, you may have a flash hot shoe: an electrical contact that enables you to connect an external flash to the camera. External flash units are generally more powerful than on-camera flash units. With an external flash unit, you can use what is known as "bounce flash." With bounce flash, the external flash unit is angled toward the ceiling or a wall. The resulting illumination is more diffuse and eliminates harsh shadows in areas such as under the subject's chin. Shadows on the wall are also diffused, resulting in a more pleasing picture.

Another option available on many digital cameras is Night Portrait mode, or Slow Synch Flash mode.

Use Slow Synch Flash

1. Mount your camera on a tripod.

2. Switch to one of your camera's creative modes.

3. Enable the camera flash.

4. Compose the picture.

5. Tell your subject to remain perfectly still while the camera records the picture.

6. Press the shutter button halfway. This focuses the scene and causes the flash unit to fire. This initial firing of the flash is used by your camera to compute the amount of light the flash adds to the scene. Your camera may show a message while it computes how long the shutter must remain open to faithfully record the background.

7. Press the shutter button fully to record the image.

Use External Flash

1. Connect your external flash unit to the camera hot shoe.

2. Compose and shoot the picture.

Enhance Your Images with Filters

If your digital camera has threads on the front of the lens mount, you can use photographic filters to enhance your photos. Filters can warm an image, cool it down, tint an image, and so on. The diameter of the threads on the front of your lens determines the size of the filters you purchase for your camera. A polarizing filter is a handy accessory, which cuts down glare from reflective surfaces like a pool of water. A polarizing filter will also make the sky look bluer. Figure 3-13a shows a scene without a polarizing filter, and Figure 3-13b shows the same scene with a polarizing filter. Notice how the clouds stand out and the sky is bluer in the scene photographed with the polarizing filter. You can find polarizing filters and other popular filters at your local camera store. Table 3-1 lists some of the popular filters and their uses.

(a) *(b)*

Figure 3-13: *A scene photographed without a polarizing filter (a). The same scene photographed with a polarizing filter (b).*

TABLE 3-1: *Popular Lens Filters and Their Usage*

FILTER TYPE	DESCRIPTION
Color compensating	Warms or cools an image. Warming filters are designated by the numbers 81 and 85, while cooling filters are designated by the numbers 80 and 82. Warming filters add an orange tint to an image, and cooling filters add a blue tint to an image.
Neutral density	Reduces the amount of light reaching the image sensor. Use a neutral density filter when you want to photograph a scene using a wider aperture (low f-stop number) or a slower shutter speed. Popular neutral density filters are ND2X (which reduces exposure by one f-stop) and ND4X (which reduces exposure by two f-stops).
Polarizing	Reduces glare from reflective surfaces. Polarizing filters also increase the saturation of the sky, which makes it look bluer and provides good contrast with clouds in the scene.
Skylight	Used to reduce the bluish cast that appears in images photographed in daylight. This filter adds warmth to an image. Skylight filters are a wise investment as they protect expensive camera lenses from dust and scratches.

CAUTION

Do not over-tighten or cross-thread a filter when screwing it on a lens.

TIP

You can purchase a filter wrench for most popular filter sizes at a well-stocked camera shop. You use a filter wrench to remove a filter you've inadvertently over-tightened.

Use Filters to Enhance Images

1. Select the desired filter.
2. Gently screw it into the threads on the front of your lens.
3. Compose and shoot the picture.

QUICKFACTS

CREATING HOMEMADE SOFT-FOCUS FILTERS

With a bit of ingenuity, you can create your own filters. For example, to create a soft-focus effect, take a pair of white pantyhose (one with a run that is not needed anymore) and cut a section that's larger than your lens. Cut a small hole in the center of the pantyhose filter. This cut-out area will be in clear focus, while the surrounding image will have a dreamy soft-focus look.

You can also take an inexpensive skylight filter, screw it on the lens mount, and smear the outer perimeter of the filter with thin film petroleum jelly. This will also give you a soft-focus effect. Apply more petroleum jelly to the outer perimeter for a graduated transition from clear focus to blurred color. Do not apply any petroleum jelly where you want your subject to be in clear focus. The results of this technique can be seen in the adjacent image. If your camera doesn't have a screw-in filter mount, you can place a piece of glass coated with petroleum jelly over the lens. Whichever method you choose, be careful not to get any petroleum jelly on the camera. In fact, it's a good idea to carry a package of moist towelettes in your camera bag to remove any dirt or grime that may have accumulated on your hands before handling your camera.

Use the RAW File Format

Many high-end and most digital SLRs have the capability to capture images in the RAW format. A RAW image is pure digital data, exactly what the image sensor recorded; the image is not processed. Therefore, no compression is applied to the image and you have more data with which to work. Many beginning photographers shy away from capturing in RAW format because it takes up a lot of room on the memory card, and most camera manuals don't give clear-cut instructions on how to work with RAW images after capturing the picture. After you download the image to your computer, you can view it using the viewer supplied by the camera manufacturer. You can then correct for any deficiencies in exposure, correct white balance, sharpen the image, and so on. After processing the image, save the image as a JPEG or TIFF file. Processing images captured in RAW format will be covered in Chapter 7.

Capture Images Using the RAW Format

When you capture images in RAW mode, you'll have to switch to one of the creative modes: aperture mode, shutter mode, or manual mode. Some cameras offer a program mode as well. When you capture an image in RAW mode, your camera creates two files: the image and a thumbnail of the image.

1. Turn the camera mode dial to select the desired creative shooting mode.
2. From the camera menu image size section, choose the **RAW** format.
3. Capture the image.

4. Download the image to your computer.

5. View the image on the associated viewer, as shown in Figure 3-14.

6. Export the image in the desired file format for further processing.

Figure 3-14: You view RAW images with software supplied by the camera manufacturer, or with the Photoshop CS Digital RAW application.

Chapter 4

Shooting Landscapes and People

After you learn the basic functions of your digital camera, you're ready to capture digital images of your world. You can use your digital camera to take compelling pictures of landscapes, friends, and loved ones. In this chapter you'll learn techniques to photograph landscapes, people, and animals.

Capture Your World Digitally

A digital camera is a wonderful thing. You can carry it with you wherever you go and capture the moments, places, and people that are important in your life. Time is a fleeting thing, and some events can never be recaptured, but after you click the shutter on your digital camera, you know within a second or so whether you have a compelling picture of the moment or not. In the upcoming sections, you'll learn some techniques that will help you digitally capture the special times in your life.

Photograph Landscapes

Photographing landscapes requires developing an eye for interesting scenes and then creating a dramatic composition. You don't have to be in a hurry when photographing a landscape, but you do need to plan your photograph. First and foremost, photograph the landscape during the golden light of the morning or late afternoon. Other than the time of day, you can take your time, as landscapes are static and do not change, unless of course you want to capture atmospheric phenomena such as a brewing thunderstorm.

Photograph Scenic Vistas

When you photograph a landscape, examine the vista from all angles. Look for an interesting composition that draws your viewer into the scene. If you're serious about photographing landscapes, study the work of master landscape photographers like Ansel Adams.

1. Choose the proper composition. If you're photographing a landscape with rolling mountains, a horizontal composition works best, as shown here:

TIP

If possible, when composing a landscape scene, include objects near the camera such as blades of tall grass or flowers. Shoot the scene with the smallest possible aperture, as outlined in Step 4, and all elements in the scene will be in sharp focus.

2. If you're photographing a landscape with a tall feature, such as a towering sequoia, a vertical composition and a low camera angle will accentuate the feature, as shown in the image to the right.

3. Position the horizon. Many beginning photographers place the horizon in the middle of the picture, but you can add a sense of grandeur to a scene when you lower the horizon line, as shown below.

4. Shoot the scene with the smallest possible aperture (a large f-stop number) for the maximum depth of field. If you're shooting the scene with a point-and-shoot digital camera, choose the landscape shooting mode. If your camera has an aperture priority mode, record the scene using the mode and choose an f-stop of f/11 or greater. Refer to the "Use Preset Shooting Modes" and "Shoot Images Using Creative Shooting Modes" sections of Chapter 2. If you're shooting in dim lighting conditions, you may have to increase the ISO rating in order to achieve a fast enough shutter speed.

5. Take several photographs of the scene from different vantage points and camera angles. Remember, if you don't like an image, you can always delete it.

Photograph Skyscapes

You can also create dramatic photographs of cloud formations. When photographing a skyscape, the sky should be the predominant object in your photograph. You'll get the best photographs of clouds if you photograph early in the morning or late in the afternoon toward sunset.

- One option is to zoom in directly on the cloud formation and include no landscape elements in the picture.

  —Or—

- Photograph an interesting cloud formation at sunrise or sunset with a non-distracting foreground as shown in the following illustration.

TIP

If you own a polarizing filter, use it to increase contrast when photographing skyscapes. Twist the outer ring of the polarizing filter to deepen the blues in the sky.

QUICKSTEPS

PHOTOGRAPHING CITYSCAPES

1. Big cities are exciting places to visit—and to photograph. Most major metropolitan areas have distinguishing landmarks. New York City has the Empire State Building, San Francisco has the Transamerica Building, and St. Louis has its trademark arch. Each of these landmarks instantly triggers memories of your visit. Photographing a cityscape is just like photographing a vast landscape of plains and mountains. Set your camera to landscape mode, or if you can manually adjust the camera, choose aperture mode and the smallest aperture (large f-stop number) possible while still maintaining a high enough shutter speed to avoid blurring. Compose a view of the skyline of the city you are visiting, but try to avoid the cliché shot that appears in every tourist brochure. If you live in the city, you'll know just which shots to avoid.

2. If you're photographing a skyline, choose a horizontal composition as shown in the following illustration. Notice how the curved seawall leads your eye to the drawbridge and then the skyline of Tampa, Florida.

Continued . . .

Photograph Oceans, Lakes, and Waterfalls

Man has always been lured to the water. The sounds of waves crashing against the shore or a gurgling brook are hypnotic and soothing. You can capture the tranquility and beauty of oceans, lakes, and waterfalls with your digital camera.

Photograph Seascapes

1. When you photograph a seascape, shoot with a wide-angle lens to capture the vastness of the ocean and include other features to tie the viewer to a geographical location. Another option is to create a dramatic picture by zooming in and capturing a wave crashing into the shore. Zoom out to capture the expanse of a seascape. Include geographical features such as the following image, which shows the headland to Tomales Point at the Point Reyes National Seashore in California.

PHOTOGRAPHING CITYSCAPES

(*Continued*)

3. If a tall landmark appears in your scene, consider a vertical composition. The image to the right shows the Transamerica Building in San Francisco, with a cable car in the foreground.

4. To create a slice of life, photograph a busy city street and use a zoom lens at a high level of magnification. The image to the right depicts Stockton Street in San Francisco's Chinatown. Notice how the high degree of magnification makes the buildings appear to be closer together then they actually are.

2. Zoom in on a wave and shoot with a high shutter speed to create a wavescape as shown in the photograph to the right.

TIP

Instead of shooting directly into the sun at sunrise or sunset, turn the other way. The scene will be vibrant with golden hues from the low sun.

Photograph Lakes

Lakes can make interesting subjects for photos. The key to creating a good photograph of a lake is lighting. Your photos will be enhanced if you have interesting clouds or other subjects in the scene to direct the viewer's eye. A dock or boat is a useful object to draw your viewer into a scene, as shown in the following photograph of a sunset on a Florida lake.

PHOTOGRAPHING SCENES AT SUNRISE AND SUNSET

Whether you capture a sunrise or sunset will depend on the area in which you live, the geographical features you want to include in your picture, and your own internal clock. If you want mountains in your picture and the mountains lie to your east, you photograph a sunrise. If you want the ocean in your picture and the ocean is to your west, you photograph a sunset. If you're a morning person, you photograph a scene that looks good at sunrise; if you're a night owl, you photograph a scene that looks good at sunset.

When photographing sunrises and sunsets, your camera may have a tendency to underexpose the scene to compensate for the brightness of the sun. Your camera may have a mode for shooting sunrises and sunsets that will expose the scene correctly. If not, overexpose the scene by one or two f-stops to maintain detail. If your camera has a tendency to create a bright halo when shooting directly into the sun, hide the sun behind a tree or building, as shown in the following photograph.

Photograph Brooks and Waterfalls

When you photograph waves, you use a high shutter speed to freeze the wave. You can also use a high shutter speed to stop the motion of a brook or waterfall. However, you can also use a slow shutter speed to capture an image of a brook or waterfall, which will create graceful patterns of flowing water, as shown in the following image.

Never look directly at the sun through the viewfinder as it may damage your vision.

BEYOND THE PERFECT SUNRISE OR SUNSET

Many people believe that the once the sun goes down, the sunset is over. When you photograph a perfect sunset with billowing clouds, wait a few minutes. As the sun sinks below the horizon, it still illuminates the underside of the clouds. If you're patient, fifteen minutes to a half an hour after the sun sets, you'll see several photographic possibilities evolve as the sun paints wild colors over the clouds, as shown next. If you photograph a sunrise, the opposite is true. Arrive at the scene a half an hour before the sun actually rises about the horizon. You'll find the sun paints the clouds with wonderfully muted colors before popping above the horizon. Your camera may have a tendency to overexpose a scene before a sunrise or after a sunset, making it appear brighter than it actually is. You'll notice this when the image appears on your LCD monitor. If the scene is too bright, underexpose by one or two f-stops and then take the picture again.

Take Your Digital Camera on the Road

Digital photography can be downright addictive. With no film to buy and no film to process, there's no reason your digital camera shouldn't be a constant companion. You never know when a photo opportunity presents itself. Of course, you should always take your digital camera when you go on vacation. Vacations are special times with friends and family that fade quickly from memory once you're back into your daily routine. However, you can relive your vacation at any time by reviewing your digital journal of the trip.

Before Your Vacation

1. Research your trip ahead of time:
   - Review websites for the cities you intend to visit and note any places you would like to photograph.
   - Review travel brochures to see how other photographers have photographed the area you intend to visit.

2. Pack your camera gear:
   - Be sure you have extra memory cards or a laptop computer to which you can download your images.
   - Pack extra batteries.
   - Remember to pack your battery charger. If you're traveling overseas, make sure your battery charger will work in the countries you are visiting. Otherwise purchase a voltage adapter.
   - Pack your camera lens cleaning equipment.
   - If desired, pack a tripod. Note that you can purchase lightweight tripods that can be packed in luggage.
   - Pack your camera gear in your carry-on luggage; otherwise, rough baggage handlers may damage your camera. And there's always the possibility your camera may get stolen by a less than honest baggage handler or security person.

Photograph Your Vacation

1. Photograph subjects or buildings that people will associate with the places you visit. Remember to examine the scene and photograph it from a unique vantage point to add your own creative touch to the photos. For example, the following image shows the Washington Monument photographed from the Vietnam War Memorial.

2. Include pictures of friends or relatives in front of historic landmarks or other scenic vistas. If you can, photograph people with their backs to the sun to avoid squinting faces, and remember to compensate for the backlit subjects. Compose pictures of this type so the people in the picture and the landmark are identifiable. Avoid mistakes like having the Tower of Pisa growing out of someone's head.

3. To include yourself in pictures with friends and relatives, ask a passerby who looks trustworthy to take the picture. Compose the scene first and then hand the camera to the passerby and instruct him or her on how to release the shutter.

4. Capture the special moments. For example, if your vacation involves air flight, take a picture of a loved one catching a catnap before boarding a flight.

5. Try to plan visits to major tourist attractions on off days. This helps you avoid fighting long lines and crowds of people. As an added benefit, you get pictures of the tourist attraction without massive throngs of tourists in every shot.

6. If you're staying in the same city for several days, photograph historic landmarks or unique vistas at different times of the day and in different weather conditions. Clouds and the setting sun can add ambiance to what would otherwise be a bland photo.

7. Make your visit coincide with any interesting parades or activities that take place in the city you plan to visit. You can generally find this type of information on the city's website. Arrive at the event early so you can claim a good spot on the sidelines that will enable you to photograph the event without including other spectators.

Photograph People in Public Places

When you travel to a distant locale, people pictures help document your visit. For example, a visit to San Francisco's Chinatown would not be complete without capturing images of the Chinese men and women playing Mah Jong.

However, most people shy away from having their pictures taken by strangers. Here are a few techniques you can use to catch spontaneous pictures of people.

1. Photograph the scene from a distance using a zoom lens, as shown in the illustration to the right.

2. If you own a camera with an LCD viewer, sit at a nearby table, open the LCD viewer and compose the scene. People won't think you're taking their picture if you're not looking at them through the main viewfinder.

3. Do not use the camera flash, as this is a dead giveaway you're taking a picture.

Photograph Friends and Family

A digital camera is a wonderful way to capture the special moments and times of the important people in your life. Many people contrive an unnatural pose when a camera is pointed at them, while others are just natural hams in front of the camera. Knowing your subject is the key to getting a good picture. If your subject is uncomfortable in front of the camera, back up and give them some room. Keep your finger poised on the shutter button, and click it when you see something you like. And if someone asks you not to take their picture, respect the person and do as they request.

Capture Digital Images of Friends and Family

1. Compose your picture, remembering to place the main subject at a point of interest. For more information on composing images, refer to the "Compose the Photograph" section in Chapter 3.

2. Choose an interesting vantage point. For example, when photographing a young child, position the child on a chair so you're photographing from the same level or slightly lower than the child.

3. Avoid taking photographs of people when they're eating.

4. When photographing an event such as a wedding or birthday, take several shots to capture the range of emotions.

5. When at an informal event such as a party, keep on the move and take photos from several vantage points.

6. Avoid distracting backgrounds. Your friends and family are the stars of your images.

7. When taking a picture of two people, zoom in tight and compose the picture so that the subject's heads are aligned with points of interest (the Rule of Thirds).

Capture a Digital Portrait

1. Step away from the subject.

2. Rotate the camera 90 degrees and frame the subject vertically.

3. Zoom in to achieve the desired composition. You can zoom in for a head and shoulder portrait, as shown to the right, or zoom in tight and capture just the person's face and part of his or her hair. The latter is known as an extreme close-up.

4. Talk to your subject to relax her while you're photographing her. Ask her some questions about what she likes, her family, or how she spends her spare time. A relaxed subject will give you more natural pictures.

5. Make sure the subject's eyes are in focus. Remember, the eyes are the windows to the soul. If possible, compose the photograph so one of the subject's eyes intersects a point of interest (the Rule of Thirds) as shown in the photograph to the right.

TIP

You'll get more pleasing portraits if you use available light instead of relying on the camera flash. Photograph your subject seated in a chair staring out a window on a cloudy day. The soft light won't create any harsh shadows and helps hide facial features such as wrinkles and crow's feet.

TIP

If you must use flash when shooting a portrait, put a piece of tissue paper in front of the flash. This will diffuse the light resulting in a more flattering portrait.

TIP

If you're photographing a really large group, take the pictures outdoors if feasible.

QUICKSTEPS

CAPTURING IMAGES OF THE FAMILY'S BEST FRIEND

1. Dogs and cats are treasured family members and can be wonderful subjects for your digital photographs. Dogs and cats have totally different personalities. Dogs are content to follow their masters everywhere, whereas cats can be somewhat aloof. Big dogs can be the subjects of wonderful action shots as they jump high to catch a Frisbee. A cat will strike a contemplative Zen-like pose as the feline gazes into the distance for minutes at a time. That is, until you grab a string and dangle it in front of the cat's face. Avoid photographing your pets with flash. Number one, they don't like the bright light and will shy away from you the next time you point a camera in their direction. Number two, dogs and cats are also subject to red-eye, but in the case of dogs and cats, the reflection from the animal's retina makes your pet's eyes look like they're glowing.

2. Photograph large dogs against a plain background. If you photograph a large dog with black fur against a dark background, the animal will be lost in the picture.

3. If you're photographing a pet with dark fur, photograph the animal against a light background.

Continued . . .

Photograph a Group of People

1. Find a unique vantage point from which to photograph your scene. For example, when you photograph a group of people at a table, avoid the head-on shot from the end of the table. If you stand on top of a chair or on the second or third rung of a stepladder and photograph the group from above, you'll create a more interesting photo.

2. Take control of the situation and tell your subjects where you want them to stand. If you're photographing a large group of people, tell the taller people to move to the back and position small children in the front of the photo. You can also ask the first row of people to kneel.

3. As you compose the scene through the viewfinder, be aware of any gaps between people. Also make sure all of your subjects are visible in the viewfinder. It's okay to crop off part of a subject's arm, but avoid cropping off someone's facial features. If necessary, back up a little.

4. Tell your group to strike different poses to avoid the "police lineup" syndrome where everyone is ramrod straight and their gaze is fixed on the photographer.

5. Take several photos to make sure you catch everyone looking their best. Remember, you can always delete the bloopers where some of your subjects had their eyes closed or were in mid-yawn when you snapped the picture.

Photograph Nature

If you live near a wildlife reserve or a remote lake, you can use your digital camera to capture wonderful images of nature. You can also capture images of wildlife at your local zoo. Each type of photography is equally challenging, and you'll face some obstacles when trying to capture the perfect image. When photographing wildlife, use a bit of common sense and keep your distance. Rely on your camera zoom lens to get close-ups. Even the most docile animals will attack if they feel threatened or provoked. Shooting wildlife with a camera can be very rewarding. This is a very different type of hunting where you end up with a trophy picture instead of depleting the population of the species.

CAPTURING IMAGES OF THE FAMILY'S BEST FRIEND

(*Continued*)

4. Take photos of your cat staring out the window. The soft diffuse lighting will highlight the animal's fur and provide wonderful catch-lights in the cat's eyes, as shown here:

5. Zoom in on your pet and choose the largest possible aperture (small f-stop number) to blur the background.

CAUTION

Always leave yourself an escape route in case wild animals sense your presence. Keep within sprinting distance of your vehicle or a building so you have easy access to a safe haven if the animals you are photographing begin acting aggressively. Never photograph a mother and her cubs unless you're using a telephoto lens from a long distance.

Photograph Wildlife and Nature

1. If you're photographing animals like bears or deer, stay downwind of the animals so your scent won't give you away.

2. If possible, photograph the animal from higher ground.

3. Switch to aperture priority mode if your camera has it, and choose a large aperture (low f-stop number). If you own a point-and-shoot digital camera, switch to portrait mode. Either method will create a blurry foreground and background with the animal you are photographing in sharp focus, as shown next. Alternatively, if you're photographing rapidly moving animals, switch to shutter priority mode and choose a shutter speed fast enough (1/500 second or faster) to freeze the animal in motion.

4. Zoom in on the animal and compose the scene.

5. Shoot the picture.

QUICKSTEPS

TAKING A DIGITAL SELF-PORTRAIT

If your camera is equipped with a self-timer, you can take a picture of yourself. Your camera's self-timer may be menu driven, although some cameras have external controls for this feature. The self-timer counts down a given interval before taking the picture. This gives you time to move into the frame. Some cameras have two self-timer time selections: generally two to five seconds, and ten seconds. The self-timer can also be used to include you in a photograph with friends or family.

1. Position your camera on a tripod.

2. Enable the self-timer feature.

3. Compose the picture.

4. Press the shutter button.

5. Walk into the frame and wait until the shutter opens and closes. Most cameras with a self-timer feature will flash a light as the camera counts down. The flashes become more rapid just before the shutter opens, which is your cue to smile for the camera.

TIP

If the zoo will allow it, carry a lightweight three-foot aluminum stepladder and take your pictures from the next to the top rung. This allows you to shoot over the heads of other spectators and over fences.

Capture Images in a Zoo

With a bit of planning and persistence, you can take pictures of animals at a zoo that look like they were taken in the wild. You do face obstacles when you photograph at a zoo, however. For one, there is the fencing that keeps the wildlife within the zoo. You also have other spectators viewing the animals. To capture realistic wildlife images from a zoo, you'll have to minimize both obstacles:

1. If possible, plan your visit to the zoo on a weekday to minimize the amount of spectators you'll have to work around, especially if you're visiting a famous zoo like the San Diego Zoo.

2. Choose a vantage point with a natural background. If possible, shoot from a high vantage point. This will enable you to shoot over fences.

3. If you're forced to photograph through a chain-link fence, zoom in, or use a telephoto lens. Switch to aperture priority mode and choose a large aperture (low f-stop number), which will throw the chain link out of focus and make it less apparent. When shooting through a fence, you'll also have to manually focus on the animal. Otherwise the camera will focus on the fencing as it is the nearest thing to the camera.

4. Zoom in on the animal.

5. Compose and shoot the picture.

Photograph Birds

You can create dramatic pictures of nesting birds and birds in flight with your digital camera. You can capture pictures of birds in your own backyard if you have a bird feeder, or you can photograph them at a local lake.

1. To photograph stationary birds, choose aperture priority mode and then choose a large aperture (small f-stop number). If your camera doesn't have an aperture priority mode, choose portrait mode.

CREATING AN ABSTRACT SELF-PORTRAIT

If your camera is equipped for night photography without flash, you can create a unique self-portrait by placing your camera on a tripod and selecting aperture priority mode (Av on most cameras). Select the smallest aperture (largest f-stop number) to ensure a lengthy exposure. Press the shutter button and then walk into the frame. Stay in the frame for a few seconds and then walk back toward the camera. The end result will be a ghostly image of yourself through which the background can be seen. This partial transparency occurs because you're only in the frame for part of the exposure. To add a bit of variety to the otherwise static image, move a small penlight back and forth while you're in the frame, as shown to the right.

TIP

Photographing a bird in flight is a matter of luck. Point your camera where you think the bird will be and then wait for the scene to unfold. Alternatively, you can track a bird in flight with your camera and then snap the picture. Synchronize the motion of your camera with the bird's flight and then squeeze the shutter.

2. To photograph birds in flight, switch to shutter priority mode and then choose a shutter speed of 1/500 second or higher to capture an image similar to the one shown next. If your camera isn't equipped with a shutter priority mode, choose sports mode. If you're photographing a bird over a clear lake, you'll have the added bonus of a mirror reflection of the bird in flight.

3. Zoom in on the bird.

4. Shoot the picture.

Photograph Aquatic Wildlife

You can capture wonderful photos of sea life without getting wet. If you live near a major city that has a public aquarium, you can take photos that look like they were taken underwater. Most public aquariums have displays with natural coral and sponges, complete with fish. The trick is to capture the image without the glare from the aquarium glass. There are two ways you can do this. You can use a polarizing filter (see the "Use Filters to Enhance Images" section in Chapter 3) and dial out the glare. Or, if you don't own a polarizing filter, experiment with different angles until you find one that minimizes the glare.

1. Disable the camera flash.

2. Attach a polarizing filter to the lens mount and dial out the glare. Alternatively, move to a position where the glare from the aquarium glass is at a minimum.

3. Choose an ISO setting that will enable you to photograph using a shutter speed of 1/250 second or faster.

4. Compose your picture.

5. Press the shutter button when a fish swims into the scene, as shown in the following image.

If you live near a tidal pool, you can capture compelling photographs of small sea creatures during low tide. Use a polarizing filter to cut out the glare from the sun. If the water's clear, you'll capture wonderful images.

> **TIP**
>
> When photographing sea life through aquarium glass, make sure the glass isn't capturing reflections of people behind you, or of yourself.

Chapter 5
Shooting Action Sequences

When you take a photo of a person or landscape, you have a captive subject, and lighting and composition become your main concerns. However, when you want to use your digital camera to take pictures of people or objects in motion, you have different challenges. In addition to dealing with lighting and composition, you have to portray motion in your image. In this chapter, you'll learn several techniques for capturing motion with your digital camera.

Capture Action with Your Digital Camera

It would be wonderful if you could freeze time for a brief second to capture a moving object with your digital camera, and then with a snap of the fingers, resume time. In essence that's what your finished image is in most cases, a slice of time where you've captured the essence of motion, be it an athlete caught in midflight while vaulting the pole in a high jump or a batter in midswing.

If you've used a film camera to photograph action, you may think you can use the same techniques, and you're almost right. Digital cameras are close to their film bearing brethren, but digital cameras have to think after you press the shutter button. Therefore *you* have to think ahead in order to capture a wonderful action scene such as the one shown in Figure 5-1, instead of a blurry, unrecognizable image.

Figure 5-1: *You can capture action shots such as this with your digital camera.*

Deal with Shutter Lag

Every digital camera has what is known as shutter lag. This is the amount of time between when you press the shutter button and when the camera actually captures the picture. The reasons for this are the myriad functions the camera performs after you press the shutter. The camera focuses the subject and then replaces the current contents of the image sensor (the last picture you took) with the subject you are photographing. The problem is exacerbated when the camera is focusing on a rapidly moving object. There are a couple of ways you can overcome shutter lag.

1. Press the shutter button halfway to pre-focus on an object that is equidistant from the camera to the area where you will photograph your subject in motion. Alternatively, you can switch to landscape mode or infinity, which increases the depth of field. If you enable landscape mode, your camera may revert to a slow shutter speed. If this is the case you'll have to pan the camera with the subject as outlined in the upcoming "Pan the Camera" section. Another alternative is to use your camera's manual focus mode to focus on the area where your subject will appear.

2. Anticipate the shutter lag and press the shutter button an instant before the action you want to capture comes into frame.

3. Reduce to a lower image quality unless you're going to print your images. It takes your camera longer to record a large image with the highest quality. Therefore a lower image quality will reduce shutter lag.

4. Enable your camera's continuous focus mode if it's so equipped. In this mode, the camera continually focuses on an object moving toward or away from you.

5. Enable your camera's continuous shooting or burst mode. This mode enables you to snap a series of pictures as long as the shutter button is held down. The images are stored in the camera memory buffer. Once the buffer is full, you will have to wait for it to empty before you can continue taking pictures. Cameras with continuous or burst mode are capable of capturing three to nine images per second depending on the camera manufacturer and model.

6. Make sure your camera is not in standby mode when the action is fast and furious, as it will take your camera a second or two to wake up when you press the shutter button.

Pan the Camera

If you shoot with a high enough shutter speed, you can freeze action. However, there are times when you need to track a subject before taking the picture. For example, if you're photographing a bird in flight, you synchronize the motion of the camera with the bird and then snap the picture at the desired moment as shown in Figure 5-2.

Figure 5-2: ***Pan the camera to capture images of subjects in motion.***

1. Switch to continuous focus mode if your camera is equipped with this feature. If not, switch your camera to landscape mode or infinity.

2. Plant your feet firmly, align the moving subject in your viewfinder, and zoom in to the desired degree of magnification.

3. Press the shutter button halfway to establish focus.

4. As the subject moves toward you, twist your torso so that your moving subject remains centered in your viewfinder. As the subject comes closer, you'll have to move faster to keep the subject in frame.

5. Press the shutter button when the subject is at the desired point.

Create a Sequence of Images

When you want to capture a sequence of images, such as a tennis player serving or returning a volley, you can use your camera's burst or continuous mode. When you shoot in burst mode, the camera continues recording images as long as you hold the shutter button, or until your camera memory buffer is full. Shooting a sequence of images is a wonderful way to record an exciting action sequence.

1. Choose the menu item or press the button on your camera that enables continuous or burst shooting mode.
2. Switch to continuous focus mode if your camera is so equipped.
3. Press the shutter button halfway to focus on the subject.
4. Press the shutter button fully and hold it to create a sequence of images, as shown in Figure 5-3.

TIP

If your camera does not have continuous focus mode and the subject is moving toward you, choose landscape mode or infinity to assure the greatest depth of field.

*Figure 5-3: **Capture motion with a sequence of images.***

Capture the Essence of Motion

Images of athletes and animals in motion depict grace, agility, and power. When you see images of animals in motion, with details such as sinewy muscles and rippling fur, it's almost like being there. There are a couple of ways you can create compelling pictures of objects in motion with your digital camera. The actual method you use depends on your subject. When you're photographing

QUICKFACTS

STEADYING THE CAMERA

When you're working with a zoom lens at extreme magnification or a high-powered telephoto lens, the slightest camera shake is magnified and can result in an unclear picture. You also run the risk of a blurry image when you photograph with a slow shutter speed. A tripod is the ideal solution for steadying a camera. However, tripods are cumbersome and can limit your mobility, especially when you need to be mobile to capture the action. With a bit of practice, you can learn to steady the camera and get sharper pictures. To steady the camera, plant your feet firmly with one foot slightly in front of the other. Your feet should also be spread slightly apart, similar to the legs on a tripod. Cradle the underside of the camera lens with one hand and firmly grasp the camera body with the other. Position your arms close to the side of your chest. Before taking the picture, inhale and then slowly squeeze the shutter button while remaining still. If you're shooting a vertical composition, plant your feet firmly and steady the camera by placing one arm close to your chest, as shown to the right.

a subject such as a pole vaulter springing over the high bar, you can freeze the action because it's readily apparent your subject is in motion. However, when you photograph an object like a racecar traveling at well over 100 MPH, freezing the action makes it look like you snapped a picture of a car parked on the track. The next two sections show you how to photograph both types of objects.

Photograph Rapidly Moving Subjects

When you photograph a subject such as a downhill skier or a pitcher unleashing a blazing fastball, your goal is to freeze the motion. A photograph of a skier with flakes of snow flying from the tips of his skis makes it readily apparent that the skier is traveling rapidly.

1. If you're using a point-and-shoot camera, switch to sports mode.

2. If you're using a high-end digital camera or a digital SLR, switch to shutter priority mode and choose a shutter speed of 1/1000 second or more. You may have to increase the ISO rating to achieve a shutter speed fast enough to freeze the action.

3. If the subject is traveling toward you, press the shutter button halfway to establish focus. If your camera is not equipped with a continuous focus mode, pre-focus on an object equidistant to the place where your subject will be when you capture the image. Alternatively, switch to continuous focus mode if your camera is so equipped.

4. Press the shutter button fully to capture the desired image.

Blur Image Backgrounds to Enhance Motion

When photographing rapidly moving vehicles, the practice of using a high shutter speed goes right out the window. Sure, you freeze the action, but you also freeze everything else, including the rapidly rotating wheels and tires. The image you end up with looks like you took a picture of a parked vehicle. The solution is to use a slow shutter speed and pan with the subject.

1. Switch to shutter priority mode.

2. Choose a slow shutter speed of 1/60 second.

3. Pre-focus the camera on a subject that is equidistant to the point at which you will take the picture.

Continued . . .

QUICKSTEPS

STEADYING YOUR CAMERA WITH A MONOPOD

For another alternative to steady a camera, you can investigate a monopod. A monopod is a lightweight alternative to a tripod. This device is similar to a walking cane and, as the name implies, has one (mono) leg (pod) and a mounting screw you attach to your camera's tripod mount. A monopod has a series of interlocking tubes that you extend or retract to adjust the device to the desired height. Many monopods also feature a retractable three-legged foot that can be accessed by unscrewing the mount at the bottom of the tripod.

1. Connect the monopod to the bottom of your camera.

2. Loosen the locking collars, extend the monopod to the desired height, and tighten the locking collars.

3. Extract the monopod's retractable foot if so equipped.

4. Plant your feet firmly and cradle the camera as outlined in the previous sidebar. In essence, your two feet form the second and third legs of a tripod when used in conjunction with a monopod.

Continued . . .

TIP

When using a monopod to steady the camera while photographing in a low-light situation, switch to a higher ISO setting. This enables you to choose a higher shutter speed.

4. When the vehicle comes into view, center it in your viewfinder and begin panning the camera with the vehicle as outlined previously.

5. Press the shutter button fully when the vehicle reaches the desired position. Remember to continue panning after your press the shutter button. An image taken using this technique is shown next.

Photograph a Sporting Event

You can capture wonderful images of sporting events with your digital camera. For example, if one of your children is on a school team, you can capture one of the team's events for posterity. When you photograph a local sporting event, you usually don't have to contend with huge crowds. You generally have unlimited access, which enables you to take photographs from many different vantage points. And that's the key to capturing good images at a sporting event: take a wide variety of pictures from different vantage points.

5. Compose your picture and then press the shutter button halfway to focus on your subject.

6. Inhale and then slowly press the shutter button fully to take the picture as shown in the following illustration.

TIP

Most monopods have a wrist strap. Use this in conjunction with your camera's neck strap to ensure the camera doesn't go crashing to the ground while you're changing memory cards. After you photograph a scene with a monopod attached to your camera, collapse the extension tubes and tighten the locking collars before moving to another location. Alternatively, unloosen the mounting screw and take the camera off your monopod.

Another possibility is photographing a major sporting event such as a football game or an automobile race. When you photograph a major sporting event, you will have to contend with crowds, and you won't be given carte blanche access to certain places. However, with a bit of creative thinking, you'll be able to take memorable pictures. The upcoming sections list a few techniques you can use to photograph local and major sporting events with your digital camera. When you photograph a sporting event, you're telling a story. Photograph all stages of the event from beginning to conclusion. You can also capture compelling images of the athletes' awards ceremony or victory celebration.

Take Photographs Before the Event

When athletes prepare for competition, they perform time-honored rituals. For example, marathon runners stretch and then loosen up by jogging. At an automobile race, racecars are prepared in the paddock, as shown in Figure 5-4,

Figure 5-4: **Take behind-the-scenes pictures before the event starts.**

GETTING THE LAY OF THE LAND

If you can arrive early to the sporting event, you can scope out interesting vantage points ahead of time and create a plan of action. If you do a bit of planning beforehand, you'll end up with some wonderful shots.

1. If you're photographing a local football game, see if you are permitted to take photographs from places other than the grandstands.

2. If you're photographing a major event in a stadium, choose your seat wisely. If you purchase tickets for the event online or through the mail, see if you can find the seating chart for the stadium online. Alternatively, you can ask the event promoters to mail you a seating chart. Whatever type of event you attend, if possible, scope out the venue ahead of time for the best photographic vantage points.

3. If you are allowed to move freely from your seat during the event, look for places where you can photograph the event with an unobstructed view. Photographing from a high vantage point with a zoom lens can give you dramatic pictures. On the other hand, if you can photograph an event at the same level as the athletes and you can gain an unobstructed view, you can create compelling photographs.

4. Look for any vantage points where you can capture dramatic photographs of the athletes, such as the tunnel from which football players exit the locker room.

while the drivers prepare their equipment and don fireproof clothing. When you capture behind-the-scenes images, you capture more of the ambience of the event, rather than the typical cut-and-dried static photos taken by noncreative photographers.

1. Arrive at the event early.

2. If you're photographing a local event such as a high school football game, ask for permission to photograph the athletes as they prepare for the event. You can capture some wonderful images of athletes adjusting shoulder pads and strapping on kneepads, helmets, and so on. Another possibility is a close-up of an athlete's eyes as photographed through a helmet.

3. When photographing close-up images of athletes, switch to portrait mode. Alternatively, switch to aperture priority mode if your camera is so equipped and shoot with the largest possible aperture to create a limited depth of field. Your goal is a crisp picture where the athlete is in sharp focus but the background is blurred.

4. If the sport you are photographing has a support team, such as cheerleaders at a football game or a pit crew at an auto race, photograph them as they prepare for the event.

5. Photograph principals in the sport such as the head coach conferring with the team, giving them final instructions before the heat of battle. If possible, zoom in to capture the range of emotions and the bond between the coach and athletes.

6. If you're photographing a team event, watch a practice session or warm-up. While watching the practice session, pay attention to the different athletes to get a feel for which athletes are more aggressive than others, which take risks, and which are rivals. This information enables you to track the athletes that will provide the most memorable shots.

7. Moments before the event starts, photograph individual athletes from a distance. Zoom in tight on the athlete's face to capture the mask of concentration as the athlete mentally prepares for the event.

Capture Images of the Event

The type of event you're attending determines what vantage points and access you'll have to shoot photographs. If you're attending a stadium event, you'll be somewhat hampered by other spectators. However, if it is possible to leave your seat during the event, you can take pictures from different vantage points.

1. Photograph the start of the event. For example, if you're photographing a basketball game, zoom in and take a photograph of the tip-off. If you're photographing a football game, take a wide angle shot of the opening kickoff, capturing the image a second or so after the ball leaves the kicker's foot.

2. Switch to continuous mode if your camera is so equipped. This enables you to take a sequence of images when the action gets hot and heavy; for example, when a soccer player rushes towards a one-on-one with the goalie.

3. Switch to sports or continuous focus mode if your camera is so equipped.

4. Zoom in on the athletes and follow the action.

5. Press the shutter button halfway while following the action through your viewfinder. Pan the camera to follow an athlete or group of athletes, and then press the shutter button when something interesting happens.

6. Photograph the event from different vantage points if possible. The following image shows a racecar speeding down the front straightaway as shot from high in the grandstands with a high-powered zoom lens.

7. Keep an eye on the sidelines for reactions from the coaches and teammates on the bench when someone scores.

8. If you're photographing a timed event, take several pictures of the action as the clock winds down.

9. If you're photographing an event such as a triathlon, bicycle, or automobile race, take several pictures as the athletes cross the finish line, as shown in Figure 5-5.

*Figure 5-5: **Capture a sequence of images of athletes as they cross the finish line.***

TIP

When taking finish line photos, switch to continuous mode if your camera is so equipped. Press the shutter button to capture a sequence of images as the athletes cross the finish line.

TIP

You can create memorable photos if you take pictures of athletes moments after the end of a competition. For example, a photograph of a marathon runner seconds after he crosses the finish line shows the toll a grueling physical competition takes on an athlete.

Capture the Thrill of Victory and the Agony of Defeat

You can also capture some wonderful images after the event ends. Photograph the athletes at the awards ceremony. If a friend or relative receives a trophy, you can present them with a wonderful keepsake of their smiling face as they hold the trophy high in the air. At an automobile race, get close to the winner's circle and capture images of the winning driver smiling and spraying the crowd with champagne. Take photographs of the losing team as well to capture the full range of emotions, from victory to defeat.

Photograph an Automobile Race

If you're photographing an automobile race, the venue will determine how you photograph the event. If you're photographing a race on an oval track, you'll be photographing from the grandstands during the event and perhaps from the pits prior to the event. Use your camera's optical zoom to get as close to the action as possible. If the event promoters permit you to leave your seat and photograph through the fence, you can capture some close-ups of the cars as they zoom by. Or take pictures of team members preparing for a pit stop, as shown here:

QUICKSTEPS

USING BLUR CREATIVELY

If you're fortunate enough to photograph a world-class event such as the Tour de France, where the cyclists often exceed 30 MPH in sprints, you can capture wonderful photographs of the cyclists by panning, as outlined previously. However, if you're photographing athletes or cyclists that are not moving rapidly, you can blur both the athlete and the background to create an artistic impression of motion.

1. Switch to shutter priority mode.

2. Choose a slow shutter speed of 1/15 second or less.

3. Pre-focus the camera on a subject equidistant to the place where you'll take your picture.

4. Pan the camera with the athlete.

5. Press the shutter button to capture an artistic impression of motion, as shown to the right.

If you're photographing a road race on a natural terrain course, roam from corner to corner. Many tracks have spectator mounds, which are wonderful vantage points for photography. When you photograph a road race, you can capture the essence of speed if you pan the camera as outlined previously. Shoot with a shutter speed of 1/60 second and pan as the car races towards a hairpin curve to capture images like the one shown next.

How To...

Chapter 6

Beyond Point-and-Shoot Photography

Creative people stretch the envelope. Whether you own a point-and-shoot digital camera, high-end digital camera, or digital SLR, you can take your photography to the next level by combining the techniques from previous chapters with the techniques you'll learn in this chapter. In this chapter, you'll learn advanced composition techniques, how to photograph during adverse conditions, and how to improvise to capture a picture in adverse conditions.

Advanced Composition

The difference between a humdrum photograph and an outstanding photograph is composition. Vacationers take pictures of stunning vistas like El Capitan in Yosemite National Park, yet their images pale in comparison

QUICKFACTS

RULE OF THIRDS IN PORTRAIT PHOTOGRAPHY

The Rule of Thirds as it pertains to landscape photography was covered in Chapter 3. When you take a portrait of a person, you should also think about composition. When you create a portrait of a person using the Rule of Thirds, you create a more compelling photograph. Another thing you should consider when taking a portrait of a person is rotating the camera 90 degrees. The image to the right is a vertical composition where the little girl's right eye is aligned on a center of interest.

TIP

Kneel to take the picture from a lower vantage point, so you are looking up toward the geometric form. Remember to keep the camera level, otherwise you'll distort vertical lines, making them appear to lean inward.

to those photographed by a master photographer such as Ansel Adams. By applying a few rules of composition, you can create pictures that will be the envy of your friends and neighbors.

Use Geometric Composition

Another method you can use to create an interesting photograph is to create a geometric composition. When you size up a scene, look for geometric elements such as rectangles, triangles, or circles. A geometric composition can also include curves that lead the viewer to a center of interest that is aligned according to the Rule of Thirds.

Use Rectangles and Squares as Compositional Elements

One of the keys to a successful photograph is examining a scene and using elements of the scene as part of your composition. If you have a scene with strong geometric elements such as rectangles or squares, use them to your best advantage when composing the scene:

1. Walk around the scene and look for strong geometric elements. With a bit of work you'll find geometric forms in key points of your scene.

2. Look for interesting objects to draw your viewer into the rectangular element that is your center of interest.

3. Take the picture. Figure 6-1 shows a geometric composition with a strong rectangular element. Notice the rectangular shape created by the sign and supports. The curve of the anchor draws the viewer into the scene and the staff of the anchor is a strong vertical element that leads the viewer toward the sign. The rectangular shape frames the entry to the ship behind.

Figure 6-1: **Use geometric elements to add pizzazz to your pictures.**

Compose a Scene with Circular Elements

Another geometric element you can use to compose your scenes is a circle. When you compose a scene with circular elements, you can look for repeating patterns or a series of circular elements. If you compose a scene with a series of circular elements, try to compose the scene so that one of the circular elements is positioned on a center of interest (Rule of Thirds). The viewer's eye will be drawn toward that element and be naturally drawn to the other circles in your picture.

1. Analyze the scene and look for the strongest circular element.

2. Compose the scene so that the strongest element intersects a point of interest (Rule of Thirds).

If you're taking a head and shoulders portrait of someone with glasses, have them hold a circular object such as an antique pocket watch or magnifying glass. Tell your subject where to position his or her hand and the object to create a center of interest according to the Rule of Thirds. The viewer's eye will be drawn from the circular object to the subject's glasses.

3. Take the picture. The following image is a scene that is strongly dominated by circular elements. The viewer's attention is first drawn to the pretty purple flowers and then naturally flows to the circular lily pads. The lily pads are bordered by a school of gently undulating koi fish, which leads the viewer's eye back toward the circular lily pads.

Compose a Picture Using Repeating Elements

If you use your digital camera frequently, you're always on the lookout for new and interesting things to photograph. You can create interesting pictures of repeating elements such as sailboat masts or windmills:

1. Analyze the scene from all angles.

2. Align the repeating elements so that they draw your viewer into the picture.

3. Choose a vantage point that makes it readily apparent you want to draw your viewer's attention to the repeating elements.

4. Switch to aperture priority mode and choose a small aperture (large f-stop number) for the greatest depth of field. If your camera is not equipped with aperture priority mode, switch to landscape or infinity mode.

5. Take the picture. The following image shows two vintage hot rods. The viewer's eye is first drawn toward the shiny chrome wheel of the first car. The picture is composed so that the wheel, fender, and mirror of the black car mirror those elements from the first car.

Use Curves to Compose a Photograph

You can use curves to draw a viewer into your scene, as outlined previously. You can also pose a subject so that his or her body parts form gentle curves that attract the viewer's attention. A photograph showing a person with a gracefully

TIP

You can also use curves when photographing people. You can direct your subject to move into a position where the curve of her neck and jaw form a compositional element in the picture. You can also direct your subject so that the curls in her hair align along a center of interest, or you can direct your subjects so that their arms form graceful, natural-looking curves in the picture. Don't overdo it, however, or the pose will look awkward, or it may appear as though your subject's arm is broken.

QUICKSTEPS

ADDING PERSPECTIVE TO A PHOTOGRAPH

When you're photographing a landscape or a cityscape on a clear day, you can see for miles. You can capture this sense of distance in a photograph when you add perspective. You add perspective when you compose the scene. For instance, if you're photographing a long city street, you can use the roofline, which appears smaller in the distance to show perspective. When you photograph a long city street, the cars parked on the side of the road appear to converge in the distance.

1. Zoom all the way out, or switch to a wide-angle lens if you're photographing with a digital SLR.

2. Switch to aperture priority mode and choose a small aperture (large f-stop number) to ensure maximum depth of field. Switch to landscape or infinity mode if your camera doesn't have an aperture priority mode.

3. Compose the scene so that you've got either tall buildings in the foreground, or a wide city street. If you're photographing buildings, the top of the building nearest the camera should fill the frame vertically or extend slightly beyond it to add a sense of grandeur to the picture. If you're shooting a city street, make sure the bottom of the frame shows the street from side to side for the same reason.

Continued . . .

TIP

When photographing perspective, take the picture from a kneeling position or get closer to the ground to exaggerate the height of the buildings.

arched back, curved limbs, and a tilted head is more interesting than one in which the person is ramrod straight. If you're patient, birds will adopt graceful poses for you. Figure 6-2 shows a bird whose neck is curved in a classic S-curve. Figure 6-3 shows a close-up of a statue with a reverse S-curve.

Figure 6-2: *If you're patient, birds will adopt graceful poses.*

Figure 6-3: *You can also find S-curves in statues and sculptures.*

ADDING PERSPECTIVE TO A PHOTOGRAPH

(Continued)

4. If possible, get a tall person walking across the road as you shoot the picture. This will help enhance the feeling of perspective, especially if you shoot the photograph from a kneeling position.

5. Take the picture. The following image shows a young lady photographed on a set of railroad tracks. The photographer was kneeling while somebody else was looking to make sure no trains were coming. Notice how the converging lines of the railroad tracks add a wonderful sense of perspective to the image.

TIP

When you photograph an individual from a bird's-eye view, make sure you're far enough away from the subject that you don't have to zoom out or use a wide-angle lens, which will distort the person's features.

Compose a Photograph from Unique Vantage Points

Many beginning photographers shoot from eye level, which can result in perfectly wonderful photographs. However, when you shoot from above a subject, your photograph takes on a whole new meaning. The same is true if you photograph an object such as a vehicle or tall building from a crouching or kneeling position. The vehicle or building looks larger than life. Landscapes also benefit when you shoot from a crouching or kneeling position. The landscape looks more majestic, and if there are any mountains in the scene, they appear to be higher.

Shoot a Photograph from a Bird's-Eye View

If you're photographing a crowded street or a group of people, shoot from above the crowd. The resulting picture will be more interesting. Photographing a street scene from a rooftop or the window of a second-story hotel room will give you a whole new perspective. You'll be able to see more people from the elevated vantage point than if you photograph the scene from street level. You can also create interesting portraits of people from high vantage points. Landscapes are also great candidates for photographing from a bird's-eye view.

The image to the right was photographed from a scenic overlook above Muir Beach in California. The photograph was taken on an exceptionally clear day, and you can see details from the outskirts of San Francisco in the distance.

QUICKSTEPS

TILTING THE CAMERA

Many photographers think there are only two orientations for a picture, landscape (horizontal) or portrait (vertical). But you can add a creative touch or a sense of whimsy to a photo if you tilt the camera diagonally. This technique is effective when you have strong diagonal elements in the scene.

1. Analyze the scene from different vantage points.

2. Look for any dominant diagonal elements such as the gable end of a roof or a person's leg.

3. Tilt the camera so that the strong diagonal is parallel to one of the edges of the camera frame.

4. Alternatively, you can look for horizontal elements such as the roadway in the following image. Tilt your camera so that the horizontal is diagonal from the top edge of the frame on one side to the bottom edge of the frame on the other side.

5. Press the shutter button fully to capture the image.

TIP

If you're photographing in an area that's relatively free of obstacles, look through your viewfinder as you move about the scene until you see the perfect composition.

Shoot a Photograph from a Snail's-Eye View

If you want something to look larger than life, photograph the subject from a crouching or kneeling position. When you do this, make sure you're far enough away from your subject so you don't have to tilt the camera to fit the subject or scene in the frame. If you do, you'll distort the perspective of the scene and edges of buildings will appear to lean inward. The photographer was prone and very close to the car when he photographed the next image. The wide-angle lens made the headlight and front air intake look huge, which was just the effect the photographer was after. The sinuous curve of the fenders draws the viewer further into the picture.

Frame Your Subject

If you're photographing a person or an object, you can use architectural elements to create a frame around the person. When you create a frame around a subject, you leave no doubt in the viewer's mind what you are photographing.

1. Find a doorway, gate, or other architectural aspect with which to frame your subject. You can frame the subject's entire body with an architectural element such as a doorframe or gate, or you can use foliage such as palm fronds to frame your subject. You can also frame a body part, such as a subject's head. In the image to the right, tree trunks and foliage frame a couple gazing out at a lake. The splash of light on the woman's hair and the man's red cap draws the viewer's eye into the scene.

2. Tell your subject the pose you'd like them to adopt. Just because you're framing them in a doorway doesn't mean they have to stand bolt upright. Have your subject move his or her arms and legs to adopt a graceful pose. If the doorway is open, the subject can turn sideways and lean against the doorway resting one foot on the ground and angle the other into the doorjamb while turning his or her face toward the camera. The subject's arms can be draped gracefully or artfully crossed underneath his or her chest. The image to the left is a picture of a young girl whose head is framed in a windowpane.

LOOKING FOR NATURAL VIGNETTES

Being observant is one of the key traits of a good photographer. If you've ever seen a photograph that has been transformed into a vignette, you know that the subject is the center of attention, and there is an elliptical area around the subject that gradually fades to black. Sometimes Mother Nature creates wonderful vignettes with light and shadows. With keen observation skills, a digital camera, and a bit of good luck, you can frame a subject in a natural vignette and create an image similar to the following.

TIP

Make sure your tripod is level.

Create Soft Portraits and Still Lifes

Your on-camera flash can help you capture images when there isn't enough available light to photograph with a fast shutter speed. However, on-camera flash is a very harsh light. When you photograph a person with on-camera flash, the resulting photograph will show every wrinkle and imperfection on the person's face. Plus when you work with on-camera flash, you'll have to deal with red-eye. A better lighting solution for portrait photography is available light. You'll have to use a tripod because of the slow shutter speed, but you'll get a better picture as a result.

Photograph by Window Light

You can create wonderful portraits by using the available light from a window. The light is generally diffuse, unless it's early in the morning and the window faces the east. If there are curtains over the window, the light is filtered even further, resulting in a wonderfully soft diffuse light that is perfect for taking portraits.

1. Mount your camera on a tripod.

2. Position your subject so that the light pouring through the window illuminates one side of his or her face.

3. Disable the camera flash.

4. Set the camera in auto-timer mode.

5. Move and adjust the tripod as needed to compose the scene. If desired, use the tripod controls to rotate the camera 90 degrees to achieve a vertical composition.

6. Press the shutter button halfway to establish focus. When you press the shutter button, you'll also be able to see the required exposure through your camera viewfinder or LCD monitor.

7. Remind your subject to sit perfectly still while the camera is recording the exposure. If you notice that the required exposure is going to be several seconds, tell your subject to remain still until you tell them the camera has finished taking the picture.

8. Press the shutter button fully. After you press the shutter button, the camera begins counting down. Do not touch the camera until the picture appears on your LCD

monitor, otherwise you'll shake the camera and get a blurry picture. Diffuse window life is also wonderful for still life images, as illustrated by the colorful picture of fruit shown next. Notice how the soft light nicely models the fruit without causing harsh shadows.

Fill in Shadows

The only problem you may encounter with shooting images with available light is that one side of your subject's face may be in deep shadow. This problem is exacerbated if you're relying solely on window light and the room in which you are photographing is dark. You could turn on a light, but then you're dealing with light sources with different color temperatures, and your camera may have a hard time getting the white balance correct. The solution is to reflect some light into the shadow areas of the scene. You can purchase a reflector from a local camera store, or you can build one yourself. If you purchase one from a

camera store, you'll need a 42-inch round reflector if you're photographing the person from head to toe. If you're only photographing the person's head and shoulders, you can get by with a 22-inch reflector. Reflectors are white, silver, or gold in color. You can also create your own reflector by purchasing a large piece of white poster board or a piece of Styrofoam. Figure 6-4 shows an assistant aiming a 42-inch reflector at the subject to be photographed. The reflector has white fabric on one side and gold on the other. The reflector fabric unzips and is reversible. The reverse fabric colors are black (which is used to deepen shadows) and silver. The reflector collapses and fits in a 16-inch diameter bag.

Figure 6-4: Hand-held reflectors bounce light back into shadows.

Fill Shadows with a Reflector

1. Set your camera on a tripod and position your subject as outlined previously.

2. Set the camera in auto-timer mode.

3. Have a friend or family member hold the reflector and angle it so that the light is caught by the reflector and bounced back into the shadow side of your subject's face.

4. View the scene through the viewfinder and tell your assistant which way to move the reflector. You'll be able to see the difference through the viewfinder.

5. Press the shutter button halfway to focus the scene.

6. Press the shutter button fully and release. The camera counts down and records the picture. The image to the right was captured using available light under a tree. An assistant aimed a gold reflector at the model to bounce some light back into the heavy shadows on her face. The gold reflector also added warmth to the image, which was photographed on an overcast day.

Photograph by Candlelight

Candlelight is another wonderful light source for available light photography. The light from a candle is warm and golden, much like the light you'll find early in the morning or late in the afternoon.

TIP

Your camera may have a tendency to focus on the candle as it's the brightest object in the scene. Have the person you're photographing move the candle out of the frame. Shine a flashlight on the subject and then pre-focus the camera on your subject. After establishing focus, have your subject reposition the lighted candle.

1. Dim or extinguish any lights in the room and then mount your camera on a tripod.

2. Switch to aperture priority mode and choose the widest aperture (smallest f-stop number) available for your camera (or lens, if you're using a digital SLR).

3. Seat your subject and place a lighted candle in front of him or her.

4. Switch to auto-timer mode.

5. Zoom in on your subject and compose the picture.

6. Press the shutter button halfway to establish focus.

7. Press the shutter button fully and release. Your camera counts down and then takes the picture.

TIP

If the resulting candlelight portrait shows heavy shadows on the sides of your subject's face, take the picture again, this time with two additional candles for side lighting. The candles can be in or out of the frame.

Deal with Adverse Conditions

Just because there's rain on the horizon or it's nighttime, don't pack your camera thinking you won't get a shot. If you're only a fair-weather daylight photographer, you're missing some wonderful opportunities for compelling pictures. When the weather's cloudy or overcast, the light is wonderfully diffuse. And when it rains, you get some lovely reflections of street lamps and buildings on the wet asphalt. If you're really lucky, after a rainstorm you can get a picture-perfect rainbow with everything but the proverbial pot of gold. In the upcoming sections you'll learn some techniques for taking pictures in less than ideal conditions.

TIP

If the exposure is long enough, you can move a flashlight back and forth across the side of your model's hair to paint some light into the picture.

COPING WITH ADVERSE LIGHTING

When you photograph in adverse conditions, you're generally dealing with adverse lighting conditions. This can be anything from dealing with lighting that is uneven, low lighting, or heavy shade. The following list shows some remedies for adverse lighting:

- Use fill-flash to fill in shadow when photographing in heavy shade or when the subject is backlit.

- Use a reflector to bounce light back into the shadow side of a subject's face.

- Increase the ISO setting to achieve a higher shutter speed.

- Use a tripod or monopod to steady the camera when photographing at slow shutter speeds in low lighting situations.

- When you use a tripod to photograph a low light scene, use the camera auto-timer to avoid camera movement when you press the shutter button. Alternatively, use a camera remote switch to trigger the shutter without touching the camera.

- Use your car headlights to add additional light when photographing in low light situations.

- Use an off-camera flash with a swivel head and angle the flash at the ceiling to bounce light on your subject and avoid harsh shadows.

NOTE

When taking a portrait of someone at night, you should use the camera flash only as described in the "Use Slow Synch Flash" section in Chapter 3. Most digital camera flash units are not powerful enough to capture night scenes.

Photograph at Night

After the sun goes down and total darkness sets in, you have some wonderful picture taking opportunities available. If you're vacationing in an exciting city, capturing images of the street lights and tourist attractions will provide memories for years to come. In order to photograph night scenes, you'll need to increase the camera ISO rating, and/or use a tripod. When you increase the ISO setting, you may end up creating a bit of digital noise. However, sometimes a little digital noise can add to the excitement of a bustling night scene.

1. Mount your camera on a tripod. Alternatively, you can steady the camera using the methods described in the "Shoot Low Shutter Speeds without a Tripod" section of this chapter.

2. If desired, choose a higher ISO setting to increase camera sensitivity.

3. Disable the camera flash.

4. Switch the camera to auto-timer mode.

5. Switch the camera to aperture priority mode and choose a small aperture (high f-stop number) to achieve maximum depth of field. If your camera is not equipped with aperture priority mode, switch to landscape or infinity mode.

6. Mount the camera on a tripod.

7. Compose the scene and press the shutter button halfway to establish focus.

8. Press the shutter button fully and release. The camera begins counting down and takes the picture. The image to the right of San Francisco's Fisherman's Wharf was photographed using the steps from this technique.

PHOTOGRAPHING IN INCLEMENT WEATHER

When the weather turns really foul, your best bet is to stay inside. Digital cameras are expensive and will quickly be ruined if subjected to moisture. Plus it can be downright dangerous to photograph when a thunderstorm is nearby and the wind is howling. However, when the rain slacks to a drizzle, or ends completely, you can capture some wonderful images. If you take photographs at night after a rainstorm, the glistening pavement will create wonderful reflections of car lights, streetlights, neon signs, and so on. When you photograph night scenes during inclement weather, you'll have to steady the camera with a tripod or use a high ISO rating. The following image was photographed an hour or so after a rainstorm abated and the streets were almost dry. The camera was mounted on a tripod with the auto-timer enabled.

Photograph a Distant Thunderstorm

Electrical storms can be quite frightening when you're in one, but they can be quite beautiful when viewed from a distance and you can see lightning pop out of the billowing thunderheads. If you're patient and far enough away from the storm to be out of harm's way, you may be able to capture some fantastic images. Switch your camera to continuous shooting mode and compose the scene. When you see the far-off lightning start to pop, hold the shutter button and your camera will take several pictures. With a bit of luck, you may get an image like the one that follows.

Improvise to Capture the Moment

Photography is rewarding, but it can also be a challenge, especially when you're far away from home or photographing in a public place such as a museum. When you're on vacation, you need to pack light, which means that goodies such as your tripod and off-camera flash and other equipment that won't fit in your luggage are left languishing at home in the closet. When you're photographing in a museum, flash is often not allowed, as the intense light will damage the old paintings and other artwork. Other times you may be in a situation that calls for a reflector but yours is at home. What do you do? Improvise.

Shoot Low Shutter Speeds Without a Tripod

Sometimes you're not permitted to use a flash, such as in a museum of fine art. There are other times when you want to photograph a scene, such as a busy plaza at night, but your on-camera flash is not powerful enough to capture the entire scene. The obvious answer is a tripod. But what do you do when you've left home without one? Find something to rest the camera on so it will remain steady during a long exposure:

1. Disable your camera flash. When you disable the flash, your digital camera increases the exposure time sufficiently to capture the scene.

2. Switch your camera to auto-timer mode.

3. Position your camera on a solid surface such as a restaurant table or a park bench. If you want a vertical composition, press your camera against a solid object such as the side of a building.

4. Compose the picture and then press the shutter button halfway to establish focus.

5. Press the shutter button fully and wait for the camera to count down and take the picture. The resulting exposure may be quite long, so don't move the camera until you see the image appear in your LCD monitor. If you're holding the camera against

the side of a building to achieve a vertical composition, hold the camera as tightly to the wall as possible and remain as motionless as possible while the camera records the exposure. The following image is a horizontal composition of a night scene taken at Fisherman's Wharf in San Francisco. The camera was positioned on a stainless steel counter with the self-timer enabled. Notice the wonderful reflections in the countertop and the colorful glow from the neon signs.

TIP

If you're photographing a night scene, switch to landscape or infinity mode. If your camera has aperture priority mode, choose a small aperture (high f-stop number). The resulting exposure will be longer, but more of the scene will be in focus.

Create a Makeshift Reflector

Reflectors are wonderful ways to splash light back into the shadow side of a subject's face when you're photographing using available light without flash, but homemade reflectors made from sheets of Styrofoam are bulky and not convenient when you're vacationing. However, with a bit of ingenuity, you can find items that you can use as substitutes for reflectors:

- Have a family member hold up a bed sheet to splash light into the shadow side of a loved one's face as you take an introspective portrait using window light.

- Use your car's removable sun reflector as a makeshift reflector. Many window reflectors have two sides, silver and gold. Use the silver side when you just need to add light to the shadow side and the gold side when you need to add some warm light to the shadow side. When the following image was photographed, someone was pointing the gold side of a car sun reflector toward the young lady to add some light to the heavy shadows on the left side of her face. The gold side of the reflector was used as it also added warmth to the image, which was photographed on a cloudy day.

- Have a friend or family member angle a white beach towel to catch the sunlight and reflect it toward a person you're photographing under a beach umbrella.

- Seat your subject on a white sheet or blanket with her back to the light source. Drape another sheet or blanket over a chair or have a friend or family member hold the sheet. Move the sheet or blanket to bounce light back into the shadows. The blanket that the subject is sitting on will reflect additional light.

TIP

An extra-large white T-shirt can be used when you need to reflect light back into a person's face.

Chapter 7

Editing Your Digital Images

Taking pictures is fun. Before digital cameras, you had to wait for the film to be processed before you saw the images. With digital cameras, you see the images immediately in the LCD monitor. After you take the pictures comes another fun part of the process: editing. The editing application I'll cover is Photoshop Elements, which for all intents and purposes can function as your digital darkroom. This chapter shows you how to get your images into your computer and prepare them for printing, distribution via e-mail, or website viewing.

Get the Images Out of Your Camera

Before you can share your images or see full-sized versions of them, you must get them out of the camera and into your computer. The following sections show two methods for transferring images from camera to computer: the first

Create a master folder for all of your digital images. Create subfolders for pictures you took on a specific date and label the folders in a manner so that you can instantly tell what pictures are stored in the folder. For example, Seattle_Pix_101804 indicates that the pictures were taken in Seattle on 10/18/2004. If you label all of your photo folders, you won't have to spend hours searching through folders with illogical names for your prized vacation pictures.

The transfer from camera to computer will go faster if you are connected to a USB 2 port.

uses the USB cable supplied with most digital cameras, while the second uses a card reader, which is a relatively inexpensive accessory you can purchase at any store that sells digital cameras.

Transfer Images to Your Computer

Your digital camera comes equipped with a USB port on the camera and a USB cable. When you connect the cable from your camera to an available USB port on your computer, you're ready to start transferring images. When you transfer images in this manner, you are using camera battery power. In this regard, make sure the battery is fully charged before downloading images.

1. Start your computer and create a folder where you want to store the images.

2. Connect your camera to the USB cable supplied by your camera manufacturer.

3. Connect the USB cable to an available USB port on your computer, as shown next. What happens after you connect the camera depends on the operating system you

use. Windows XP opens a dialog box with suggested actions. Click to open a folder. If you're using a Macintosh, the default option will be to launch iPhoto and open the images in that application. Disable this option if you're using Photoshop Elements as your image editing application. After disabling this action, your Macintosh OS will recognize the camera as a removable hard drive.

4. Select all of the images.

5. Drag and drop the images from the folder you created when you connected your camera to the computer, or if you're working on a Macintosh, drag the images from the removable hard drive into the folder you created in Step 1.

6. Remove the camera from your system by disconnecting it from the USB cable.

Use a Card Reader

When you use a card reader to transfer images, the camera is not part of the operation. You remove the memory card from the camera and insert it directly into the card reader. The benefit of card readers is that you don't drain the camera battery. You can find a card reader that matches your type of memory card at most retailers. Most memory card readers are under $30.

1. Create a folder in which you'll store the images.

2. Remove the memory card from your camera.

3. Insert the memory card into your card reader. In Windows XP, a dialog box opens with suggested actions, as shown at right. Choose the option to create a folder to view the images. On a Macintosh, the default action is to launch iPhoto and edit the images. If you're working with Photoshop Elements or another image editing application, disable that option in iPhoto preferences, and the Macintosh OS will mount the card reader as a removable hard drive.

4. Select all of the images.

5. Drag the images from the folder (Windows) or removable hard drive (Macintosh) and drop them into the folder you created in Step 1.

NOTE

On the Windows operating system, you need to safely remove the device from your system by clicking the **Safely Remove Hardware** button in the System Tray, and then selecting your camera from the list of devices connected to your system. On a Macintosh computer, dismount the device from your system by dragging it to the trashcan.

Process RAW Images

Many high-end digital cameras can capture images in the RAW format. You do this by choosing the option from your camera menu. The camera does not process images captured in the RAW format. Instead, you get the image that the camera image sensor recorded, which therefore gives you richer colors. If your camera can capture images in the RAW format, a utility to process the images and save them as TIFF or JPEG files was included with your camera. To process the RAW images, install the software and follow the software instructions to process your RAW images. The following steps show a typical workflow for processing RAW images:

Histogram

1. Launch your RAW viewer utility. Your utility probably has a method for you to preview thumbnail images of the files.

2. Open the image you want to process. This will take some time as the utility decodes the file into a viewable image. Shown at left is an image being processed in the Canon File Viewer utility. Notice the graph in the upper-right corner of the image. This is a histogram, a graph that shows the distribution of pixels from shadow areas to highlights. If the graph is flat on the left side of the histogram, you don't have enough detail in the shadow areas of the image. If the graph is flat on the right side of the histogram, you're lacking detail in the highlight areas of the image.

3. If necessary, increase the exposure of the image, as shown in the following illustration.

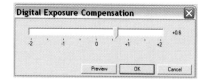

Notice the difference in the histogram when the exposure is increased. If the image was too bright (a large spike at the end of the histogram), you may be able to recover the image by decreasing the exposure.

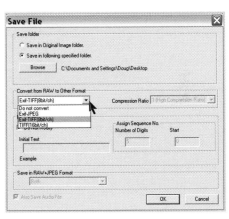

4. Continue processing the image by adjusting the contrast, color saturation, and sharpness. The image at right shows the contrast settings in Canon's File Viewer Utility.

5. After adjusting the desired settings, save the file. Your application will give you conversion options, such as those shown in the image to the right, which are the options for converting a file using Canon's File Viewer Utility. If you're going to further edit the image in an application like Photoshop Elements, choose the TIFF format, 8 bits per channel (because the current version of Photoshop Elements does not support images with 16-bit color depth).

TIP

Don't delete your RAW files after processing them. RAW image files are like film negatives. You can reprocess them as needed to create new images. Archive your RAW image files to a CD for future use.

Introduce Photoshop Elements

Whenever you edit images, you generally perform many of the same tasks. In this regard, you should adopt a workflow. Some of the most common issues you'll be dealing with when editing digital images are sharpening, color correcting, and cropping images and then saving them. The following sections outline some of the tasks that typically need to be performed on digital images and the order in which they should be performed.

Calibrate Your Monitor with a Colorimeter

Adobe Gamma is a good way to calibrate your monitor, but the results vary because the software relies on the user's subjective interpretation. A colorimeter (hardware that measures the color output of a computer screen) will give you

CALIBRATING YOUR MONITOR

When you edit images in an application like Photoshop Elements, you're making decisions based on what you see on your computer monitor. What you get when you actually print the image may be a different story. You can calibrate your monitor so that the colors you see on the screen will closely match what you get when you print the image. Adobe Photoshop Elements ships with a utility called Adobe Gamma, which leads you step by step through a process of making adjustments to the brightness, gamma, and white point of the monitor. On a Windows-based machine, you can access the Adobe Gamma utility (shown next) through the Control Panel. On a Macintosh, you can launch Adobe Gamma by choosing **Apple Menu | Control Panels | Adobe Gamma**.

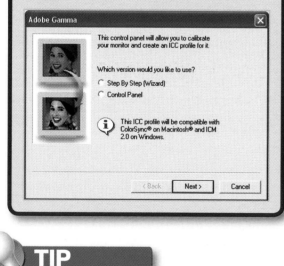

TIP

Disable any antivirus software when installing ColorPlus (or for that matter, when installing any software).

more accurate results. In the past, a hardware and software package to calibrate a computer monitor was too expensive for nonprofessional photographers. However, this has recently changed. ColorVision (www.colorvision.com) has a package called ColorPlus (Windows only), that consists of software and a colorimeter that connects to a USB port on your computer and enables you to accurately measure and calibrate an LCD or CRT monitor. As of this writing, the street price of ColorPlus is $99.99. You can purchase ColorPlus (Product Number GEU104) from CompUSA (www.compusa.com) or B&H Photo (www.bhphotovideo.com). As of this writing, you can also purchase the product online from ColorVision (www.colorvision.com) for $119 with a $30 rebate. An accurately calibrated monitor enables you to make accurate decisions when editing your photos in Photoshop Elements. What you see on the monitor will match what you get when you print the image, which means you won't waste paper or ink.

1. Install ColorPlus software.

2. Connect the colorimeter to a USB port on your computer.

3. Launch ColorPlus. After starting the application, the Introduction page shown next appears.

4. Click **Next** to open the Select Monitor Type dialog box shown next.

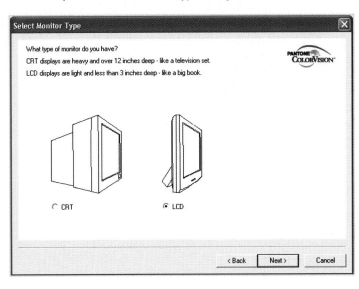

5. Select the type of monitor you are calibrating and then click **Next** to display the Measuring Display Characteristics dialog box, shown next. This dialog shows

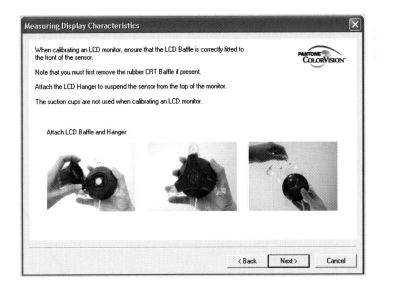

If you are calibrating an LCD monitor, do not attach the suction cups to the monitor, as you may damage the screen. The suction cups are designed for a CRT monitor. If you are calibrating an LCD monitor, tilt the monitor back to ensure that the colorimeter is flat against the screen.

Monitors change over time. Calibrate your monitor at least once a month to ensure that your monitor accurately displays colors.

you how to install the proper baffle for the monitor you are calibrating. The preceding image shows the page that appears when you are calibrating an LCD monitor.

6. Attach the proper baffle to the colorimeter and click **Next** to display the Measuring Characteristics dialog box, which shows a template of the colorimeter.

7. Align the colorimeter with the template, as shown next.

8. Click **Next**. At this stage the software takes over. You'll see several screens appear in succession on your monitor. The colorimeter is taking measurements from these screens to adjust the brightness, contrast, and white point of your monitor. This process takes about 20 minutes.

9. After the colorimeter finishes its measurements, you'll be prompted to remove the colorimeter from your monitor. You can then view an image that shows the results before and after calibration. After accepting the calibration, the software writes a color profile that is automatically loaded every time you start your computer.

Launch Adobe Photoshop Elements

Photoshop Elements has a diverse selection of tools you can use to professionally edit an image. Many of the tools are intuitive, while others become easier to use as you gain familiarity with the application. The following sections will serve as an introduction to editing digital images in Photoshop Elements. To launch the application choose **Start | Adobe Photoshop Elements 2** (Windows) or click the **Adobe Photoshop Elements** shortcut (Macintosh). After launching the application, the Welcome screen shown in the following image appears. From the Welcome screen you can click a button to create a new file, browse for a file, connect to a camera or scanner, read common issues, or run a tutorial.

TIP

If you prefer to work with menu commands, you can disable the Welcome screen by clicking the **Show This Screen at Startup** check box to clear the check mark.

OPEN AN IMAGE

You can use Photoshop Elements to finesse your digital images into pixel-perfect works of art. But before you can edit an image, you must open it. This section shows you how to open an image and points out the various parts of the Elements interface.

1. Launch Photoshop Elements.

2. Choose **File | Open** to display the Open dialog box.

3. Navigate to the folder in which you store your digital images.

4. Select the image file you want to open. A thumbnail image of the file is displayed at the bottom of the dialog box, as shown next.

To display only files of a certain type, click the arrow to reveal a drop-down menu of every file type supported by Photoshop Elements. Select the desired file type, and only files of that type will be displayed in the main window of the Open dialog box.

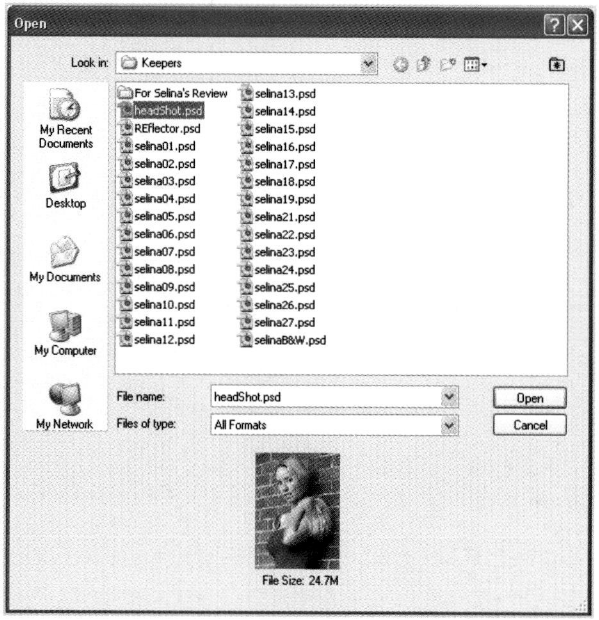

Choose a topic from the How To palette drop-down menu for quick information on how to perform a task using Photoshop Elements.

5. Click **Open** to display the image in the Photoshop Elements workspace, as shown in Figure 7-1.

BROWSE FOR AN IMAGE

The Photoshop Elements File Browser is a powerful utility, especially when you start amassing a large collection of digital images on your hard drive. When you open the file browser and navigate to a folder of images, you see thumbnail-sized images of each picture in the folder. From within the File Browser, as

Shortcuts   **Menu commands**   **Options**   **Palette dock**   **How To palette**

Tools

Document window

Figure 7-1: Edit your digital images in Photoshop Elements.

Hints palette

shown in Figure 7-2, you can open an image for editing, rotate an image, sort images, and change thumbnail size.

1. Choose **File | Browse** to launch the Elements File Browser utility. Alternatively you can choose **Window | File Browser**.

2. In the Directory window, navigate to the folder that contains the digital images with which you want to work. After selecting a folder, the File Browser displays thumbnails images of all image files in that folder.

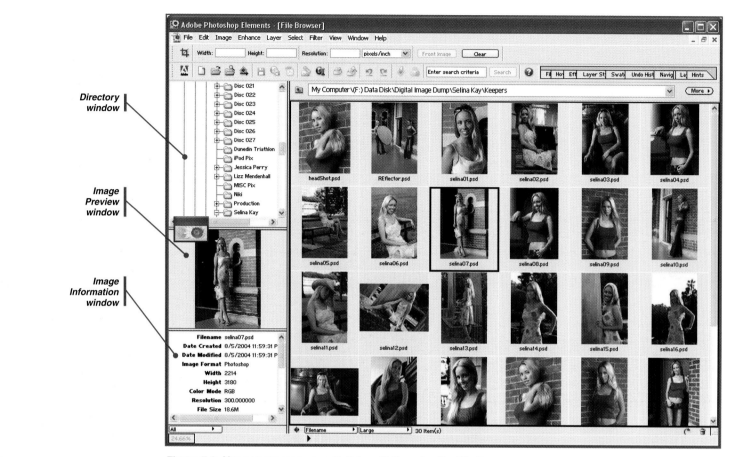

Directory window

Image Preview window

Image Information window

*Figure 7-2: **You can manage your digital portfolio using the File Browser.***

3. Select an image by clicking its thumbnail, and a small version of the image will be displayed in the Image Preview window. The information about the file is displayed in the Image Information window. Here you'll find information such as the date and time the picture was taken, the camera used to take the picture, the shutter speed, the aperture setting, and so on.

4. Double-click a selected thumbnail to open the image file in Photoshop Elements.

Sharpen an Image

Some digital cameras don't produce a very sharp image. You can sharpen images in Photoshop Elements using several different commands. However, the best choice for sharpening an image is the Unsharp Mask command, which increases the contrast of edges in your image and makes the images look notably sharper.

1. Open the image you want to sharpen.

2. Choose **Filter I Sharpen I Unsharp Mask** to open the Unsharp Mask dialog box shown at left.

3. Drag the Amount slider to the right to determine the percentage of sharpening Photoshop Elements applies to the image. Typically, a value between 100 and 150 percent works well for a high-resolution image you plan on printing, and a value between 45 and 100 works well for a low-resolution image for monitor or website viewing. As you drag the slider, you can see what the sharpened image will look like in the Unsharp Mask dialog preview window, as well as the actual image itself, if the default Preview option is selected. When you start to notice artifacts (colored specks) around the edges in the image, you've over-sharpened. Drag the slider to the left until the artifacts disappear.

4. Drag the Radius slider to determine the distance in pixels from the edge that sharpening is applied. In most instances the default value of 1 is perfect. If you decide to increase the radius, pay attention to your image. If you increase the radius too much, you'll create artifacts in it.

5. Drag the Threshold slider to determine how different pixels must be before they are sharpened. In most instances, the default value of 0 levels is perfect because it sharpens all pixels in the image. However, if you're sharpening portraits or images with large areas of flesh tones, experiment with values between 2 and 20 to avoid introducing artifacts to the flesh tones.

6. Click **OK** to sharpen the image.

Color-Correct Images

When you take a picture with your digital camera, the camera image sensor distributes the red, green, and blue pixels according to their brightness. An 8-bit image has 256 levels. Dark pixels are at the low end of the scale, while the brightest pixels are at the high end of the scale. In certain conditions, a

TIP

If you're not happy with the results, choose **Edit I Undo Unsharp Mask** before executing another command.

APPLYING THE AUTO COLOR COMMAND

To remove any color cast from an image, immediately after applying the Auto Levels command choose **Enhance | Auto Color**. The following illustration shows an image that has been color-corrected using the Auto Levels and Auto Color command in succession.

If after applying the Auto Levels and Auto Color command you notice the image does not have sufficient detail in shadow areas, choose **Enhance | Apply Auto Contrast**.

digital camera may not distribute the pixels properly, and your image may be lacking pixels at the low end of the scale. If this happens, the shadow areas of your image are not well defined. If your image is lacking pixels at the high end of the scale, highlight areas will not be well defined. You can correct for any deficiencies in levels by applying the Auto Levels command. However, when you correct levels, you may notice that the image acquires a color cast. For example, after applying the Auto Levels command, the image may look bluish or reddish. You can correct this deficiency with the Auto Color or Color Cast commands. The following image is in need of color correction:

APPLY THE AUTO LEVELS COMMAND

To correct an image that is lacking contrast, or appears washed out, choose **Enhance | Auto Levels**. After invoking the command, Photoshop Elements examines the distribution of pixels and then redistributes them as needed to correct for any deficiencies. The image at left shows the image from above after the Auto Levels command was applied. Due to the size of this illustration, you may not be able to see a color cast, and you may not notice a color cast when you preview your own images after applying the Auto Levels command. However, it's always a good idea to use the Auto Levels and Auto Color commands in succession. After you apply the command, you may still not notice a difference.

QUICKSTEPS

REMOVING A COLOR CAST

The Auto Levels and Auto Color commands usually do a good job of balancing the color in an image, but sometimes you may still notice a color cast; for example, the image may appear a bit bluish or reddish. You can use the Color Cast command to remove a color cast if you have areas in the image that you know are supposed to be black, gray, or white.

1. Choose **Enhance | Adjust Color | Color Cast** to open the Color Cast Correction dialog box shown next. Notice that the image being corrected has a red color cast.

Continued . . .

ADJUST IMAGE COLOR

You can also manually adjust the color of an image. Photoshop Elements has several commands for adjusting color. A complete tutorial on every command is beyond the scope of this book, but in this section I'll cover the Color Variations command, which makes it possible for you to adjust color with several visual references. If you'd like to find out more about adjusting color within Photoshop Elements, refer to *Photoshop Elements QuickSteps* by Carole B. Matthews (McGraw-Hill/Osborne, 2004).

1. Open the image that needs color adjustment.

2. Choose **Enhance | Adjust Color | Color Variations** to open the Color Variations dialog box. The following image shows a picture with a couple of variations adjustments applied. The left window shows the image before, and the right window shows a preview with adjustments applied.

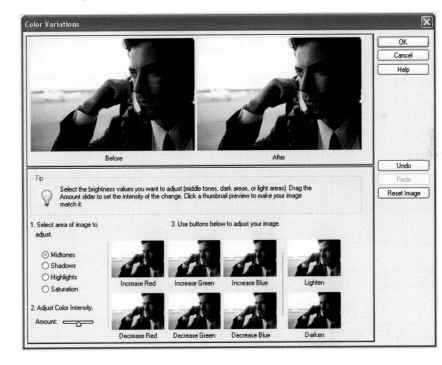

REMOVING A COLOR CAST

(*Continued*)

2. Click the **Eyedropper** and click a spot in the image that you know should be black, gray, or white. In the case of this image, the young woman's teeth are the obvious choice as they should be pearly white.

3. Click **OK** to remove the color cast. The following image shows the color-corrected image.

3. Select the color range you want to adjust.

4. Drag the Amount slider to determine how much color adjustment is applied. If you only need subtle color adjustments, drag the slider toward the left. If you need to apply larger amounts of color adjustment, drag the slider toward the right.

5. Click one of the thumbnails to have the adjusted image match the variation. After you apply a variation, the thumbnails are adjusted accordingly. If desired, you can apply additional color variations to further change the image.

6. Click the **Lighten** or **Darken** variation to lighten or darken the tonal range you are adjusting.

7. Click the **Saturation** radio button if the saturation of the colors in your image needs to be adjusted, and then click the **Less Saturation** or **More Saturation** variation, as shown next.

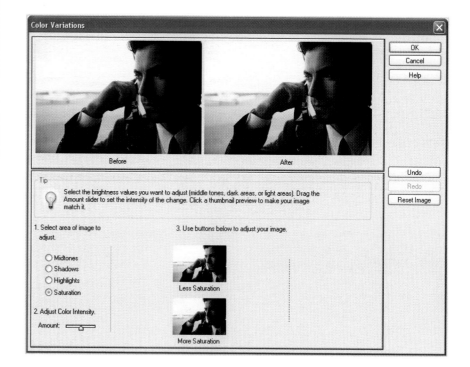

8. After the image is adjusted as desired, click **OK** to apply the variations to your image.

ADJUST BRIGHTNESS AND CONTRAST

If desired, you can manually adjust brightness and contrast. You can adjust these parameters when an image is noticeably too bright or dark or lacks contrast or if you want to create a special effect with an image.

1. Open the image you want to adjust.

2. Choose **Enhance | Adjust Brightness/ Contrast | Brightness/Contrast** to display the Brightness/Contrast dialog box, shown at right.

3. Drag the Brightness slider to the right to lighten the image; drag left to darken it. As you drag the slider, you'll be able to see the changes in your image if the default Preview option is selected.

4. Drag the Contrast slider to the right to increase contrast; drag left to decrease contrast.

5. Click **OK** to apply the change.

Adjust Lighting

When your digital camera's firmware does everything right, it's a wonderful thing. It's also a wonderful thing when the photographer knows the camera like the back of his or her hand and knows just what to do when encountering a situation where the camera firmware may not be able to compensate for a difficult situation like a bright sky in the background, or heavy shadow. If either scenario fails, the photographer (that would be you) still has options to change lighting by using Photoshop Elements Adjust Backlighting or Fill Flash commands.

ADJUST BACKLIGHTING

You use the Adjust Backlighting command when editing an image where the camera has exposed the main subject in the scene and the background is too bright.

1. Open the image you want to adjust.

2. Choose **Enhance | Adjust Lighting | Adjust Backlighting** to open the Adjust Backlighting dialog box, shown at left.

3. Drag the slider to the right to darken the background. As you drag the slider, you'll be able to see the changes to your image if the Preview check box is enabled.

4. Click **OK** to apply the changes.

ADD FILL FLASH

You use the Fill Flash command to brighten an object that is in heavy shadow. This command can recover detail in shadow areas when you should have used Fill Flash when taking the picture but didn't. You can also boost the saturation when adding fill flash.

1. Open the image you want to adjust.

2. Choose **Enhance | Adjust Lighting | Fill Flash** to open the Adjust Fill Flash dialog box.

3. Drag the Lighter slider to the right to brighten the image.

4. Drag the Saturation slider to the right to add saturation to the image, as shown at left.

5. Click **OK** to apply the changes.

Fix Images with Photoshop Elements Quick Fix

Some of your digital images may need a lot of work. If, for example, an image has lighting issues and needs color corrections, you'll need to use two of the commands covered previously. Fortunately, the Photoshop Elements designers came up with a command called Quick Fix that enables you to perform frequently used image-correction commands from within a single dialog box:

1. Open the image that needs a digital makeover.

2. Choose **Enhance | Quick Fix** to open the Quick Fix dialog box. By default the Brightness section of the dialog box is displayed first. The radio buttons in the first column of the dialog box enable you to choose the type of correction you want to apply to the image. The second column of the dialog box contains radio buttons for each adjustment in the correction category. The third displays either a button to apply an auto-correction, such as Auto Levels, or parameters for a manual correction, such

as Fill Flash. The following shows an image being enhanced in the Quick Fix dialog box. Notice the difference in the Before window on the left that shows the original image and the After window on the right that shows the image with the currently applied adjustments.

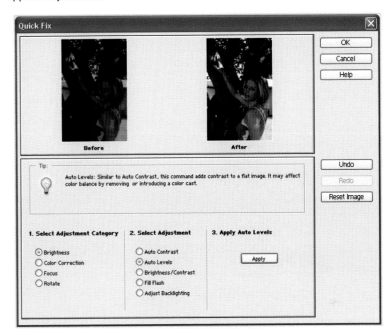

3. Chose the desired adjustment and apply it to the image.

4. Apply different adjustments in the correction category as needed. You can apply as many adjustments from a category as needed. As you apply each adjustment, the After image updates to show you the combined effect of the adjustments you've applied.

5. Continue by selecting a different correction category. The image on the following page shows the Focus corrections you can apply to an image. Auto Focus sharpens the image, while Blur softens an image. You can use Auto Focus as a quick fix in place of the Unsharp Mask command. The Blur quick fix is useful when you need to soften an image of someone taken in harsh lighting where every wrinkle and imperfection on the person's skin is visible.

TIP

Click the **Undo** button to undo the last adjustment you applied; you can click it multiple times to undo multiple adjustments. Click the **Redo** button to redo the last adjustment; you can click it as needed to redo multiple adjustments. Click the **Reset** button to restore the image to the same state as when the Quick Fix dialog box opened.

TIP

Click the **Help** button in the Quick Fix dialog box to receive precise instructions for the selected adjustment.

6. Apply additional adjustments as needed.

7. After applying the needed adjustments, click **OK** to exit the Quick Fix dialog box and apply your changes.

Create Selections

In the previous sections, you learned how to make adjustments to your digital images. However, sometimes you only need to adjust part of an image, for example, applying the Fill Flash command to just the person in the image and not the background. You can apply an adjustment, or for that matter a filter (which will be covered in Chapter 8), to a portion of an image after you make a selection. You have several tools available for selecting portions of an image, which will be discussed in the upcoming sections.

Create a Rectangular or Elliptical Selection

1. Open the image you want to edit.
2. Select the **Rectangular Marquee** tool to create a rectangular selection or the **Elliptical Marquee** tool to create a circular selection.

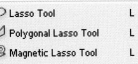

	Rectangular Marquee Tool	M
	Elliptical Marquee Tool	M

3. Click inside the image and drag to size the marquee. As you drag you'll see moving lines around the border of your selection as currently sized. The moving border is often referred to as an "army of marching ants."
4. Release the mouse button when the selection is the desired size.

Create Selections with the Lasso Tools

You can create a freeform selection with the Lasso tools. There are three Lasso tools: the Lasso tool, the Polygonal Lasso tool, and the Magnetic Lasso tool. The Lasso tools reside as a single icon on the toolbox. To reveal the Lasso tools, click the triangle in the lower-right corner of the last used Lasso tool to reveal a fly-out menu. Click the desired tool to make it the active Lasso tool.

	Lasso Tool	L
	Polygonal Lasso Tool	L
	Magnetic Lasso Tool	L

- The **Lasso** tool enables you to draw a freeform selection by clicking and dragging. If you're good with a mouse, you can create precise selections in this manner.
- The **Polygonal Lasso** tool enables you to define the shape of a selection by clicking to add points. Photoshop Elements creates a line between the two points. When you're finished defining the shape of the selection, you click the first point to close the selection.
- The **Magnetic Lasso** tool enables you to create a complex path. The tool creates points as you move your cursor over the edge of a shape.

CREATE SELECTIONS WITH THE LASSO TOOL

When you create a selection with the Lasso tool, you use the mouse to draw a freeform selection around the area you want to select.

1. Select the **Lasso** tool.
2. Click to define the starting point of your selection and, while holding the mouse button, drag around the area you want to select.

3. Release the mouse button to close the selection. An army of marching ants defines the border of your selection, as shown next:

TIP

Use the Zoom tool that looks like a magnifying glass to zoom in on the area you're selecting.

TIP

To move to another part of the document, momentarily press the SPACEBAR and then drag to the desired location. Release the SPACEBAR to revert to the previously used tool.

CREATE SELECTIONS WITH THE POLYGONAL LASSO TOOL

When you create a selection with the Polygonal Lasso tool, you click to define each point of the selection. Photoshop Elements connects the points to define the boundary of the selection.

1. Select the **Polygonal Lasso** tool.

2. Click to define the first point of the selection.

3. Click to define each additional point of the selection.

4. Click the first point to close the selection. The following image shows a fairly precise selection of the model's cowgirl hat made with the Polygonal Lasso tool.

CREATE SELECTIONS WITH THE MAGNETIC LASSO TOOL

You can make precise selections with the Magnetic Lasso tool. As the name implies, the tool develops a magnetic attraction for the edge of the object you want to select. What actually happens is the tool detects the difference in pixel color as you drag the tool over an edge, creating points as needed to define the selection. You specify the sensitivity of the tool and the distance from your cursor used to detect the edge.

1. Select the **Magnetic Lasso** tool.

2. In the Options bar shown next, which can be found below the Photoshop Elements toolbar, set the following parameters:

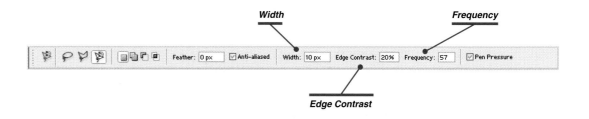

- Type a value between 1 and 40 in the Width field. This setting determines how far from your current cursor position Photoshop Elements will search for different color pixels.

- Type a value between 1 and 100 in the Edge Contrast field. High values detect edges that contrast sharply from surrounding pixels while low values detect edges with lower contrast edges.

- Type a value between 0 and 100 in the Frequency field. This determines how quickly Photoshop Elements adds points as you move your cursor over an edge. Specify a high value to anchor points more quickly.

3. Move your cursor over the object you want to select and then click to define the starting point.

4. Drag your cursor over the edge. As you trace the edge with your cursor, Photoshop Elements adds points that snap to the edges based on the specified settings as shown on the following page. When the selection is complete, the young man will be selected. The selection can be modified using one of the menu commands or tools. The selection can also be copied to the clipboard and composited into another image.

TIP

To manually create a point while using the Magnetic Lasso tool, press the **ALT** key (Windows) or **OPTION** key (Macintosh).

TIP

Press the **DELETE** key to delete the last point created. You can press **DELETE** as many times as needed to delete multiple points.

5. To close the selection, do one of the following:

- Drag your cursor over the first point and release the mouse button.

- Move your cursor toward the starting point, and then double-click to close the selection.

- To close the selection with a straight point between your current cursor position and the first point of the selection, hold down the **ALT** key (Windows) or **OPTION** key (Macintosh), and then double-click. Closing a selection in this manner is useful when you're selecting an object that ends at the border of the image, such as the torso of a person in a head and shoulders portrait.

Create Selections with Other Tools

Creating selections confounds many Photoshop Elements beginners. It can be frustrating to create a precise selection. However, with a bit of patience and practice, you can create selections of parts of the image you need to manipulate or cut a person out of one photo and insert them in another. That's why you have such a diverse choice of selection tools in Photoshop Elements. The next sections will cover the remaining selection tools.

Create Selections with the Magic Wand Tool

You use the Magic Wand tool to create a selection based on pixel color. This tool is handy if you photograph someone against a solid color wall and you want to cut the person from the background for use in another photo. You can specify how close in color the pixels must be before the tool adds them to a selection.

1. Select the **Magic Wand** tool.

2. In the Options bar, type a value between 0 and 255 in the Tolerance field. A low value selects pixels that are closer in color, while a high value selects pixels from a wider range of colors.

3. Click the color you want to select. Photoshop Elements creates an army of marching ants that defines the boundary of the selection, as shown at right.

> **TIP**
>
> If the selection isn't as desired, enter a different value in the Tolerance field and try again. Enter a smaller value if the tool selected too many pixels or a higher value if the tool didn't select enough pixels.

Create Selections with the Selection Brush Tool

You can create a selection using the Selection Brush tool. You use this tool to paint over the pixels you want to select. You can also use this tool to create a mask to protect part of an image. You'll learn to create masks in Chapter 8. When you use the Selection Brush tool, you specify the thickness of the brush as well as the brush tip.

1. Select the **Brush Selection** tool.

2. In the Options bar, choose a brush shape from the drop-down menu shown in the following image.

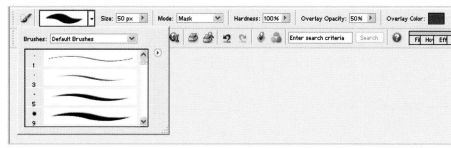

3. Select one of the following mode options:

- **Selection** paints over the pixels you want to select.
- **Mask** paints a mask over pixels you want to protect.

4. Click and drag over the pixels you want to select or mask.

5. Release the mouse button when the desired pixels are selected. The image at right shows a mask made with the Selection Brush tool. For the purpose of this illustration, the selection was made in Mask mode so it would be easier to see. If the selection had been made in Selection mode, an army of marching ants would surround the selection.

TIP

Select a soft-edged brush to gradually feather the selection into the surrounding pixels.

TIP

To remove pixels from the selection, press the ALT key (Windows) or OPTION key (Macintosh) and paint over the part of the selection you want to remove.

TIP

To quickly change the size of any brush tool in Photoshop Elements, press the right bracket key (]) to increase brush size or the left bracket key ([) to decrease brush size.

QUICKFACTS

USING A DIGITAL TABLET

You'll have an easier time creating accurate selections or working with any brush tool if you use a digital tablet. Digital tablets are devices that connect to a USB port on your computer. The digital tablet has a stylus that's shaped like a pen. You draw on the digital tablet to create a selection with one of the selection tools. The tablet is pressure sensitive, which means you can control certain parameters such as brush opacity or thickness by applying more or less pressure to the tablet. Working with a digital tablet is intuitive because most people have been using pens and pencils for the majority of their lives. It's much easier to create a precise selection using a stylus and digital tablet than it is by using a mouse. Digital tablets are sold at most stores that sell computers and, as of this writing, are priced as low as $99. The following image shows a digital tablet and stylus in use.

Edit Selections

Creating a precise selection is like sculpting. The sculptor chips away stone to find the artwork within, just as you select a portion of your image to create a great photo. However, unlike sculpting, when you create a selection and select too much or too little, you can easily add to or subtract from it. To edit a selection, do one of the following:

- To add to a selection, select the desired tool. Hold down the SHIFT key, click inside the selection, drag outside of the selection to define the area you want to add to the selection, and release the mouse button to add to the selection. You can add multiple areas to the selection as long as you hold down the SHIFT key.

- To remove pixels from a selection, select the desired tool. Hold down the ALT key (Windows) or OPTION key (Macintosh), click outside the selection, and drag inside the selection to define the pixels you want removed from the selection. Release the mouse button to complete editing the selection. You can trim multiple areas from a selection as long as you hold the ALT or OPTION key.

- To remove a selection that is no longer needed, choose **Select | Delete Selection**.

- To select the inverse of a selection, choose **Select | Inverse**.

- To feather a selection, choose **Select | Feather**. After choosing this command, a dialog box appears asking you for the number of pixels by which you want to feather the selection. When you feather a selection, the pixels in the selection are gradually blended into the pixels surrounding the selection by the specified distance.

- To save a selection for future use, choose **Select | Save Selection**. After choosing this command, a dialog box appears, prompting you for a name for the selection, as shown here. Enter the name for the selection and click **OK**.

- To load a saved selection, choose **Select | Load Selection**. After choosing this command, a dialog box appears, prompting you to select the mask to load.

Crop Images

Sometimes you get it just right and take the perfect picture. Other times, you get more than you need. You can easily remove unwanted parts of an image using the Crop tool:

1. Select the image you want that you want to crop.

2. Select the **Crop** tool.

3. Click and drag inside the image to define the area to which you want to crop the image.

4. Release the mouse button. Photoshop Elements draws a bounding box around the selected area. The area outside the bounding box (the part that will be cropped out), is 75 percent opacity black in color, as shown next.

5. To modify the crop marquee, do one of the following:

   - Click and drag a handle at any corner to resize the crop marquee width and height. Hold down the SHIFT key while dragging to resize the crop marquee proportionately.
   - Click and drag a handle in the middle of the right or left side to resize the width of the crop marquee.
   - Click and drag a handle at the top or bottom to resize the height of the crop marquee.
   - Click inside the crop marquee and drag to change the position of the crop marquee.

6. Press ENTER or RETURN to crop the image. Alternatively, you can click the **Commit** button that looks like a check mark on the Options bar.

Resize Images

When you resize an image, you are resampling an image. In other words, Photoshop Elements is taking all of the image data and redrawing the pixels so that the image is the desired size. When you choose a smaller size, Photoshop Elements does an admirable job of resizing the image. However, when you ask the application to increase the size of the image, Photoshop Elements increases the size of each pixel, which inevitably leads to degradation of the image. When you resize an image, you can also change image resolution.

1. Choose **Image | Resize | Image Size** to open the Image Size dialog box, shown here.

2. Click the **Constrain Proportions** check box. This option resizes the image proportionately, which means you need to enter only either the width or height, and Photoshop Elements will calculate the size of the other dimension to resize the image proportionately.

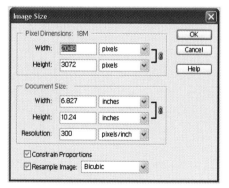

3. Type a value in the Resolution field or accept the current image resolution.

4. Type the desired width or height into the applicable field. If you type a dimension in the Pixel Dimensions section, Photoshop Elements will supply the proper dimensions for the Document Size section, and vice versa.

ABOUT FILE FORMATS

A complete dissertation of each file format supported by Photoshop Elements is beyond the scope of the book. The following list shows some of the commonly used formats for images that will be printed or distributed on the Web.

- **Photoshop (*.PSD, *.PDD)** saves an image in this format when you want to preserve masks, layers, and selections for future editing.

- **BMP (*.BMP, *.RLE, *.DIB)** saves an image in this format if you're going to use it in an application that supports it. Layers cannot be saved when you use the BMP format. This format is suitable for printing high-resolution images.

- **JPEG (*.JPG, *.JPEG, *.JPE)** saves an image in this format if you're going to display it on a website or share it with someone via e-mail. When you save an image in this format, you can specify an image quality from 0 (low quality image, small file size) to 12 (high quality image, large file size). When you specify a quality setting lower than 12, the image is compressed, which means that certain color information will be lost in order to achieve a smaller file size.

Continued . . .

Save Edited Images

After you've done all your editing and your image is pixel perfect, you can save the image for future use. Photoshop Elements has two commands for saving a file: Save and Save As. Use the Save command to save a file in its original format, and use the Save As command when you want to save the file in a different format.

USE THE SAVE COMMAND

1. Choose **File | Save** to save the image in its native format and in the same folder from which it was opened.

2. Choose **File | Close** to close the image.

USE THE SAVE AS COMMAND

1. Choose **File | Save As** to open the Save As dialog box, shown next.

ABOUT FILE FORMATS

(Continued)

- **TIFF (*.TIF, *.TIFF)** saves an image in this format if you're going to print the image. Using this format, you can choose whether to preserve layers. Preserving layers increases the file size. When you save a file using this format, you can choose whether or not to compress the image. Compressing the image achieves a smaller file size, but the trade-off is a slight loss in quality. You can take high-resolution, noncompressed TIFF images to a professional printer for quality printing. You can also print TIFF images on a personal photo-quality printer.

TIP

Immediately after you open an image you're going to edit, choose **File I Save As** and save the file as a .PSD file. This leaves your original image unaltered should something go awry during the editing process.

2. Click the down arrow to the right of the Save In field and navigate to the folder in which you want to store the image.

3. If desired, enter a new name for the file.

4. Click the down arrow to the right of the Format field and choose the desired file format. Note that each file format has different options. For the purpose of this tutorial, the file will be saved as a JPEG file.

5. Click **Save**. The format's option dialog box appears, if applicable. The image at right shows the options for a JPEG file.

6. Choose the desired options and click **OK**.

7. Choose **File I Close** to close the image.

Chapter 8

Enhancing and Correcting Images

In the last chapter, you learned how to use Photoshop Elements to do some basic image editing. But wait, there's more! After you finish your basic editing, you can enhance a photo. In this chapter you'll learn to use Photoshop Elements tools and features to add pizzazz and presence to your photos.

Work with Layers

Photoshop Elements has a powerful feature known as layers. When you open an image in Photoshop Elements, you have one layer to work with, the background layer, which is the original image. You can add as many layers as you need on top of the background layer. Additional layers can contain copies of the original image, masks, adjustment layers, and so on. You can control what effect a layer has on underlying layers by choosing a blend mode and varying the opacity of the underlying layer. The beauty of working with layers is that you can duplicate the original image on a layer and start enhancing the image on the layer. If the results are not pleasing, discard the layer and you still have your original image with nary a pixel altered.

Create a Layer

You can create layers using menu commands or from within the Layers palette. You modify layers from within the Layers palette. You can change the layer blend mode, vary opacity, change the order of layers, and so on. When you work with layers, the top layer eclipses all layers beneath it. However, elements from lower layers will be visible if you incorporate masks on the upper layers or vary the opacity of the upper layers. You can change the way the top layer looks by choosing a different blend mode. The blend mode determines how Photoshop Elements blends the pixels from the underlying layer with the pixels on the layer to which the blend mode is applied. You can also change the look of the top layer by varying layer opacity, which lets some of the underlying layer show through. Figure 8-1 shows the Layers palette of an image with several layers. For the purpose of this illustration, the Layers palette has been undocked from the Palette Dock.

Duplicate a Layer

When you apply menu commands or filters to an image, you destroy pixels. If you go too far, the image may be unusable and you'll have done a lot of work for nothing. However, if you duplicate the background layer and do all your work there, you still have the background layer as a fail-safe. Duplicating layers is also useful when you need to repair an underexposed or overexposed image.

1. Select the background layer in the Layers palette.
2. Drag the layer to the Create New Layer icon to create a duplicate layer. Alternatively you can choose **Layer | Duplicate Layer**.
3. Double-click the default layer name and type a new name for the layer as shown to the left. Naming layers is a good work habit when you'll be creating many layers to enhance an image.

TIP

To undock a palette, click the perforations to the left of the palette's name and drag it into the workspace. To re-dock a floating palette, click the perforations to the left of its name and drag and drop it into the Palette Dock.

Create New Layer

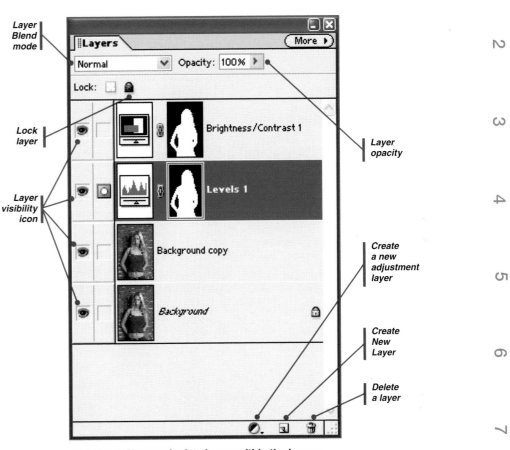

Layer
Blend
mode

Lock
layer

Layer
visibility
icon

Layer
opacity

Create
a new
adjustment
layer

Create
New
Layer

Delete
a layer

Figure 8-1: *You manipulate layers within the Layers palette.*

TIP

You can change the order in which layers are stacked by dragging a selected layer above or below its current position. You cannot move the background layer until you unlock the layer by double-clicking the lock icon.

Choose Layer Blend Modes and Varying Opacity

You control the effect one layer has upon the underlying layer by choosing the desired opacity mode. Photoshop Elements has a large variety of opacity modes. Unfortunately, a detailed discussion of all blend modes is beyond the scope of this book. The following list shows a few modes commonly used when working with digital images:

- **Normal** is the default blending mode that displays the pixels on the layer in their original form without blending pixels from the underlying layer.

- **Multiply** effectively darkens the layer by multiplying the pixels on the layer by the pixels on the underlying layer, as shown in the following image.

● **Screen** effectively lightens the layer, except where the pixels are pure black, as shown in the following image.

● **Soft Light** darkens or lightens the pixels depending on the underlying pixels. The effect is similar to shining a diffused light on the image, as shown next.

The overall effect of the blended layers depends on the opacity you choose for each layer. By default, the opacity for each layer is 100 percent. If you choose a lower value, more of the pixels on the underlying layer show through.

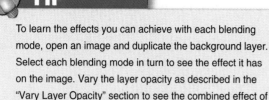
Select a Blending Mode

1. Select the layer whose blending mode you want to change.

2. Click the down arrow to the right of the currently selected blend mode to reveal the Blend Mode drop-down list, as shown to the right.

3. Click the desired blend mode to apply it.

Vary Layer Opacity

1. Select the layer whose opacity you want to change.

2. Click the down arrow to the right of the current layer opacity (100 percent by default) to reveal the Opacity slider.

3. Click and drag the slider to change the layer opacity, as shown to the left.

4. Release the slider when the desired opacity has been achieved. Alternatively, you can type a value in the Opacity text field.

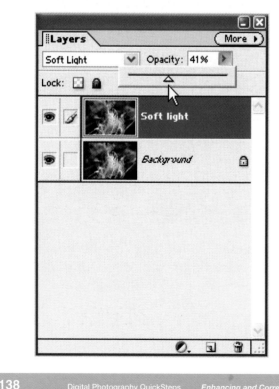

Use Adjustment Layers

You use adjustment layers to modify the image. The beauty of adjustment layers is that the original image is unchanged. The adjustment layer is pure mathematics that changes the underlying layer. You can apply many of the same edits using menu commands. However, when you apply a menu command, the edit cannot be changed after you apply other commands. Conversely, you can edit an adjustment layer at any time to fine-tune the look of your image, or for that matter, delete the adjustment layer if you don't like the effect.

1. Select the layer you want to adjust.

2. Click the **Adjustment Layer** icon at the bottom of the Layers palette.

3. Select one of the adjustment layers from the drop-down menu shown to the left.

4. To change the brightness and/or contrast of the image, choose **Brightness/Contrast** from the drop-down menu to reveal the Brightness/Contrast dialog box shown here. Then drag the Brightness and Contrast sliders to achieve the desired effect. As you drag the sliders, your image updates in real time.

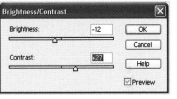

5. Click **OK** to apply the Brightness Contrast adjustment layer.

6. To change the hue and saturation of the image, choose **Hue/Saturation** from the drop-down menu to reveal the Hue/Saturation dialog box shown here.

7. Drag the Hue slider to change the overall hue of the image, the Saturation slider to saturate or desaturate the colors in the image, and/or the Lightness slider to change the lightness of the image.

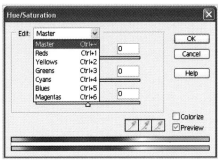

8. To change the hue, saturation, or lightness for specific colors in the image, click the down arrow to the right of the Edit field and choose the desired color range from the drop-down list shown to the right.

9. Click **OK** to apply the Hue/Saturation adjustment layer. The image on the following page shows the Layers palette with a Hue/Saturation adjustment layer applied to an image.

TIP

If you don't like the results of an adjustment layer after further editing, you can change the adjustment layer settings by double-clicking the icon. This reveals the dialog box for the adjustment layer, which makes it possible for you to alter the settings to your liking.

TIP

To delete any layer in the Layers palette, select it and drag it to the Trashcan icon in the lower-right corner of the palette.

QUICKSTEPS

CREATING A VIGNETTE

One way you can enhance a portrait of a person is by adding a vignette. You can create your own custom vignette in Photoshop Elements through the use of layers and the Elliptical Marquee selection tool.

1. Open a portrait. A head and shoulders shot is perfect for this technique.

2. Click the **Layers** tab to open the Layers palette. Alternatively, you may want to undock the Layers palette for this exercise.

3. Select the background layer and drag it to the Create New Layer icon.

4. Rename the new layer Vignette.

Continued . . .

10. Choose **Layer | Flatten Image**.

11. Save the image in the desired format.

Touch Up Photos

Digital cameras are not perfect, and neither are photographers. Sometimes camera and photographer are in synch and the result is a wonderful photo. Then there are other times when Mother Nature fools the camera or the photographer makes a wrong choice, the result being a less than perfect photo. If that less than perfect photo has redeeming value, you may be able to rescue it in Photoshop Elements. The following sections offer some remedies for common ailments.

CREATING A VIGNETTE

(Continued)

5. Select the **Elliptical Marquee** tool.

6. Create a selection around the desired section of the portrait. Remember, you can press the SPACEBAR to move the selection as you're creating it. To fine-tune the position of the selection, click inside the selection and drag to the desired location.

7. Choose **Select I Feather** to open the Feather Selection dialog box shown here. When you feather a selection, you create a region where the pixels inside the selection are gradually blended with the pixels outside of the selection. This prevents a hard edge when you're creating an effect like a vignette.

Feather Selection

Feather Radius: 150 pixels

OK
Cancel
Help

8. Enter the desired value in the Feather Radius field. This value is in pixels and determines how many pixels beyond the selection will be used for the feather. The amount you enter depends on the size of the image to which you're applying the effect. If you're creating a vignette around a large image, experiment with values 100 pixels or larger.

9. Click **OK** to apply the feather and close the dialog box.

Continued . . .

TIP

Begin painting the mask with a large brush. As you get closer to the edge of the area you want to protect, switch to a smaller brush.

Darken a Background

You can darken a background that is too bright and detracts from the main subject in your photo. Darkening a background involves using the Selection Brush tool to make a mask around your subject. The mask protects the pixels to which it is applied.

1. Open the image that contains a background you'd like to darken.

2. Select the **Selection Brush** tool.

3. In the Options bar, click the down arrow to the right of the currently selected mode and choose **Mask** from the drop-down menu.

4. Position your cursor inside the area you want to protect and begin painting. As you move the brush across the image, a red overlay appears, indicating the area that will be protected. Remember, you can resize the brush as needed by pressing the left bracket ([) key to make the brush smaller, or the right bracket (]) key to make the brush larger.

5. Continue painting the mask until the red overlay covers the area you want to protect, as shown to the right.

6. Choose **Select I Feather** to open the Feather Selection dialog box.

Feather Selection

Feather Radius: 2 pixels

OK
Cancel
Help

7. Type **2** in the Feather Radius field.

8. Click **OK** to apply the feather. After applying the feather, the edge of the mask overlay becomes blurry, indicating the area that will be feathered. If it doesn't seem large enough, repeat Step 7, but this time use a 1-pixel radius to extend the feather.

14216.JPG @ 100% (RGB)

CREATING A VIGNETTE
(*Continued*)

10. Choose **Select | Inverse**. This selects the area where the vignette will be applied.

11. Choose **Edit | Fill** to open the Fill dialog box.

12. Click the down arrow to the right of the Use field and choose **Black**.

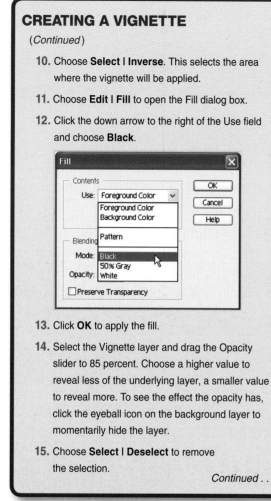

13. Click **OK** to apply the fill.

14. Select the Vignette layer and drag the Opacity slider to 85 percent. Choose a higher value to reveal less of the underlying layer, a smaller value to reveal more. To see the effect the opacity has, click the eyeball icon on the background layer to momentarily hide the layer.

15. Choose **Select | Deselect** to remove the selection.

Continued . . .

TIP

Use the Zoom tool that looks like a magnifying glass to zoom in on the subject so you cover all of the area you want to protect. When you select the Zoom tool, the mask overlay will disappear. The overlay reappears as soon as you reselect the Selection Brush tool.

9. Choose **Select | Save Selection** to open the Save Selection dialog box shown to the right.

10. Enter a name for the selection and click **OK**.

11. Open the Layers palette.

12. Click the **Adjustment Layer** icon and from the drop-down menu choose **Brightness/Contrast** to reveal the Brightness/Contrast dialog box shown to the right. When you do this, the mask overlay will disappear. Not to worry—the mask is still there.

13. Drag the Brightness slider to the left to darken the image. Don't go overboard. If you notice a halo around your subject, drag the slider to the right to lighten the background a bit. The goal is to make the subject stand out, yet at the same time appear natural.

14. Click **OK** to close the Brightness/Contrast dialog box. Your Layers palette should look as shown to the right. Notice the icon that indicates the shape of the mask.

15. Select the background layer.

16. Choose **Select | Load Selection**.

17. Select the mask you just created and click **OK**. The mask overlay appears over your subject.

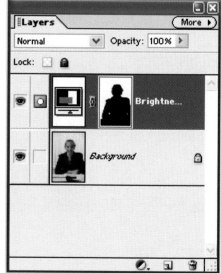

TIP

If you select more than the area you want to protect, press the ALT key (Windows) or OPTION key (Macintosh) and paint over the areas you want to remove from the mask.

CREATING A VIGNETTE

(*Continued*)

16. Click the **More** button in the Layers palette and from the Layers menu choose **Flatten Image**. This command flattens all the layers into the background layer in the image. Alternatively, you can choose **Layer | Flatten Image**. This step is not necessary if you're saving the file as a Photoshop *PSD file. Your finished image should look like the following image.

18. Choose **Filter | Blur | Gaussian Blur** to open the Gaussian Blur dialog box. A value between 1 and 3 pixels works well. The goal is to slightly blur background to draw attention to your subject.

19. Click **OK** to apply the blur.

20. Review the image. If the background is too dark, double-click the **Brightness/Contrast** icon in the Layers palette to reopen the dialog box. Drag the slider to the right to brighten the background and click **OK**. The beauty of adjustment layers is that you can edit them at any time.

21. Click the **More** button in the Layers palette and choose **Flatten Image** from the Layers menu. The following image shows the finished product. Notice how the subject stands out from the background.

Level a Photo

What seemed perfectly level when you looked at a scene through the viewfinder may not be once you get it into the computer for editing. Even professional photographers take photographs that aren't perfectly level. Fortunately, there's an easy fix for this problem.

1. Open the image that isn't level.

2. Choose **View | Grid** to display the grid, as shown next.

3. Double-click the background layer. The New Layer dialog box appears.

4. Click **OK**. In essence you didn't create a new layer, you unlocked the background layer.

5. Choose **Image | Transform | Free Transform**. Eight handles appear around the image. If you can't see the handles, click the **Maximize** icon.

6. Move your cursor toward one of the corner handles. When your cursor becomes a curved line with two arrows, click and drag to straighten the image. Align the edge of a building or something you know should be vertical or horizontal with the grid, as shown next.

> **TIP**
>
> You can also commit a change by pressing ENTER (Windows) or RETURN (Macintosh).

7. Click the **Commit** button in the options bar (it looks like a check mark).

8. Select the **Crop** tool and crop the image to remove the angular spaces that occurred when you rotated the image. The straightened and cropped image is shown next.

Fix a Photo with the Clone Tool

Sometimes bad things happen to good photographs. For example, you may have inadvertently grown a telephone pole out of your subject's head. You can fix problems like this with the Clone tool.

1. Open the image that has an object you need to clone out.

2. Select the **Polygonal Lasso** tool and create a selection around the object you need to clone out, as shown next.

3. Select the **Clone** tool.

4. Size the brush. Press the right bracket (]) key to increase the size of the brush or left bracket key ([) to decrease the size of the brush.

5. ALT-click (Windows) or OPTION-click (Macintosh) the area in your photo from which you want to clone.

6. Click and drag inside the selection to clone out the offending object.

7. Choose **Select I Deselect** to remove the selection. The image to the left shows the previous photograph after the light poles have been cloned out of the hot rod's roof.

QUICKSTEPS

CURING RED-EYE

If your digital camera does not have a red-eye reduction mode, when you take flash pictures of people, the flash reflects off their retinas and produces a red glow in each eye. You can easily correct this problem in Photoshop Elements and return the person's eyes to normal.

1. Open the image of a subject that has red-eye.

2. Zoom in on the subject's eyes, as shown next.

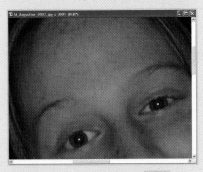

3. Select the **Red Eye brush** tool.

4. Position your cursor over the subject's eye and press the left bracket ([) key to reduce the size of the brush or the right bracket (]) key to increase the size of the brush. The brush size should be slightly smaller than the pupil of the subject's eye.

Continued . . .

TIP

By default, the replacement color for the Red Eye brush tool is black. You can change the replacement color by clicking the Replacement Color swatch and choosing a different color from the Color Picker.

Rescue Underexposed or Washed-Out Photos

If you have some dark underexposed photos, you may be able to save them using the Fill Flash command discussed in Chapter 7. You may also have some washed-out photos where the sky is too light. Don't discard these photos; you may be able to rescue them using layers and blending modes.

Rescue Washed-Out Images

1. Open an image that's overexposed or washed-out.

2. Open the Layers palette.

3. Select the background layer and drag it to the Create New Layer icon.

4. Select the new layer.

5. Change the blending mode to Multiply. This will give the image better contrast and detail.

6. If the image is now underexposed, lower the opacity of the layer. The images to the right show a before and after of a picture of morning thunderstorm clouds. The image on the top is the original, while the image on the bottom was rescued using this technique. The opacity was lowered to restore some detail to the foreground.

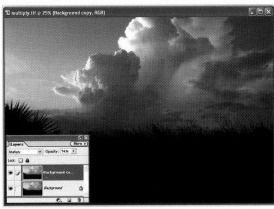

CURING RED-EYE

(*Continued*)

5. Click and drag the tool over each eye. You may have to take a couple of swipes to remove all of the red-eye. The following image shows the subject's eyes after using the Red Eye tool.

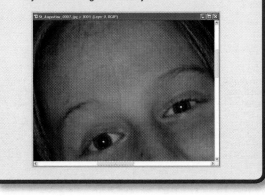

Rescue Underexposed Images

1. Open an image that's underexposed.

2. Open the Layers palette.

3. Select the background layer and drag it to the Create New Layer icon.

4. Select the new layer.

5. Change the **Blend mode** to **Screen**.

6. If the image is now too light, lower the opacity of the layer. The following images show a before and after picture of an antique car. The image on the left was underexposed, while the image on the right was rescued with this technique.

ENHANCING A SUNSET

Sunsets make wonderful photographs. However, what looked wonderful through the viewfinder may lack a little luster when you get the image into your computer. You can add life to a bland sunset by adding a layer of solid color and then lowering the opacity to achieve the desired effect:

1. Open the image in Photoshop Elements.

2. Open the Layers palette.

3. Click the **Adjustment Layer** icon and from the drop-down menu choose **Solid Color** to open the Color Picker dialog box.

4. Type **213** in the R field, **137** in the G field, and **0** in the B field, as shown next. These values create the same orange used in an 85 photographic filter, which is used to warm images.

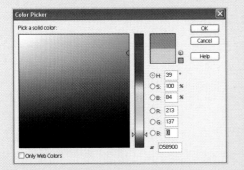

5. Click **OK**. The Solid Color adjustment layer is added to the Layers palette. Your image is solid orange.

6. Click the down arrow to the right of the current Blend mode (Normal by default) and choose **Soft Light** from the Blend Mode drop-down menu.

Continued . . .

Add a Motion Blur Effect

You can make a stationary object appear to be moving if you use the Motion Blur filter. You can also use the Motion Blur filter to add presence to an image of a moving object that appears to be standing still because you captured it at too high a shutter speed.

1. Open the image you want to enhance with the Motion Blur filter.

2. Select one of the lasso tools or the **Selection Brush** to make a selection around the object you want to blur, as shown next. The selection doesn't need to be too precise as the blur will compensate for any small areas you've missed. In fact, if you select a little more than the object, the effect will appear more natural because you won't have any sharp edges after the blur is applied.

ENHANCING A SUNSET

(*Continued*)

7. Click the down arrow to the right of the Opacity field and drag the slider until you get the desired result, as shown next.

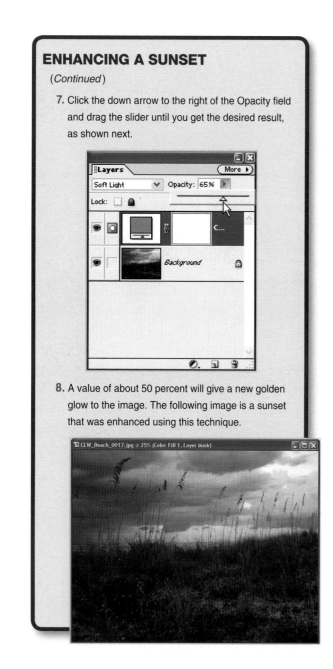

8. A value of about 50 percent will give a new golden glow to the image. The following image is a sunset that was enhanced using this technique.

3. Choose **Filter | Blur | Motion** blur to open the Motion Blur dialog box shown to the right.

4. Click the diagonal line in the circle and drag to set the angle. Alternatively, you can type the desired angle in the Angle field. As you change the angle, you'll be able to see the effects in the preview window, as well as in your object if you have the Preview check box enabled.

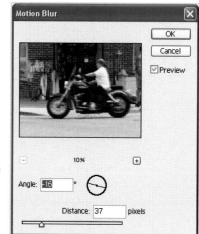

5. Drag the Distance slider to set the distance in pixels that the blur extends from the object. Alternatively, you can type a value in the distance field.

6. Click **OK** to apply the filter.

7. Choose **Select | Deselect All**. The following image shows the blur applied to the motorcyclist. The effect makes it look as though the vehicle is speeding through the scene, when in reality, the vehicle was being slowly driven around the corner.

Convert an Image to Grayscale

Digital cameras give you wonderful full-color images. However, sometimes things look better in black and white. For example, some portraits look stunning as black and white pictures. Add a vignette as outlined previously, and you've got a work of art suitable for framing.

1. Open the image you want to convert to black and white.
2. Open the Layers palette.
3. Click the **Adjustment Layer** icon and choose **Hue/Saturation** from the drop-down menu.
4. Drag the Saturation slider to –100, as shown here.

5. Click **OK** to add the Hue/Saturation layer. The resulting image should look much better than the conversion to grayscale. But wait, there's more.
6. Click the **Adjustment Layer** icon and choose **Brightness/Contrast** from the drop-down menu.
7. Drag the Contrast slider to the right until the image has the desired amount of contrast, as shown here. The value you choose is a matter of taste. Somewhere between 8 and 20 percent will yield good results.

8. Click the **More** button and choose **Flatten Image** from the Layers menu. At this point you have a perfectly acceptable black and white image, as shown to the right. If desired, you can add an artistic touch by adding film grain to the image.

9. Select the background layer in the Layers palette and drag it to the Create New Layer icon and name the new layer Film Grain.

10. Select the **Film Grain** layer, and then choose **Filter | Artistic | Film Grain**.

11. Drag the Grain slider to 10 and leave the other values at their default, as shown below.

12. Click **OK** to apply the filter.

13. Select the **Film Grain** layer and drag it to the Create New Layer icon and name the new layer Grain Blur.

14. Select the **Grain Blur** layer and choose **Filter | Blur | Gaussian Blur**.

15. Type a value of .08 in the Blur Radius text field, as shown to the right. The Gaussian Blur softens the Film Grain filter so it doesn't look so mechanical.

16. Click **OK** to apply the filter.

17. Lower the opacity of the Film Grain and Grain Blur layers to 25 percent, as shown to the right.

18. Click the **More** button and choose **Flatten Image** from the Layers menu. The converted black and white image with film grain is shown below. Compare this image to the earlier version without film grain. The differences are subtle, but they make the image look more film-like.

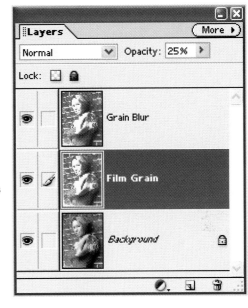

Add Text to an Image

You can add text to any image you edit with Photoshop Elements. You can add text to an image that will become a greeting card, poster, or framed artwork. You can create vertical or horizontal text using any font currently installed on your system.

Create Text

1. Open the image to which you want to add text.

2. Select the **Text** tool.

3. In the Options bar, click the **Vertical** or **Horizontal Text** icon, as shown next.

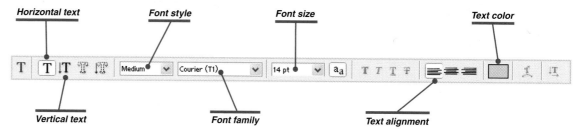

Horizontal text   Font style   Font size   Text color

Vertical text   Font family   Text alignment

4. Click the down arrow to the right of the currently selected font and select the desired font family from the drop-down list.

5. Click the down arrow to the right of the currently selected font size and choose an option from the drop-down list. Alternatively, you can enter the desired value in the text field.

6. Click the desired alignment icon to left align, center, or right align the text.

7. Click the text color swatch to open the Color Picker, shown next.

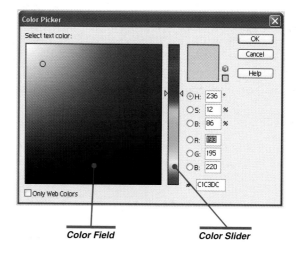

Color Field   Color Slider

8. Drag the arrows to the right of the Color slider to choose the hue and drag inside the Color field to set the saturation.

9. Click **OK** to exit the Color Picker.

10. Click inside the document and type the desired text. Photoshop Elements creates a layer for the text.

11. Select the **Move** tool.

12. Click and drag the text to the desired location.

Add a Drop Shadow to Text

1. Open the Layers palette.

2. Select the text layer to which you want to apply the drop shadow.

3. Choose **Window | Layer Styles** to open the Layer Styles palette.

4. Click the down arrow to the right of the currently selected Style Library and choose **Drop Shadows** from the drop-down list. This displays the Drop Shadows Style Library shown to the left.

5. Click the desired style to apply it to the text. The following image shows text to which a drop shadow has been applied.

Add Panache with Filters

Photoshop Elements ships with a treasure trove of filters—more than you'll probably ever use. You've already seen the results of some of the filters in the earlier section of this chapter. The following sections will show you how to use filters to add style to your images and create special effects. You can access filters from the Filter menu or from the Filters palette, shown in Figure 8-2.

Figure 8-2: You can drag and drop filters onto your images.

Create Painterly Images

Photoshop Elements has several filters you can use to add a painterly touch to your images. If you're a frustrated watercolor artist, or you like to dabble with colored pencils but just can't seem to make it work, you'll love the artistic and sketch filters. The following steps will give you an idea of what you can do with them. In this tutorial, you'll take it one step further by applying the filter on its own layer and using the Opacity control to let some of the original image shine through.

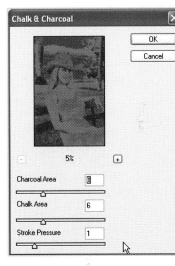

1. Open the photo you want to transform into a painterly image.

2. Open the **Layers** palette.

3. Drag the background layer to the Create New Layer icon and name the layer Chalk & Charcoal.

4. Select the second layer.

5. Choose **Filter I Sketch I Chalk & Charcoal** to open the dialog box shown above and to the right.

6. Drag the sliders to achieve to desired look.

7. Click **OK** to apply the filter to the layer.

8. In the Layers palette, set the opacity for the layer to 80 percent, as shown to the right.

9. Click the **More** button in the Layers palette and choose **Flatten Image** from the Layers menu. The image to the left shows a portrait that was modified using this technique.

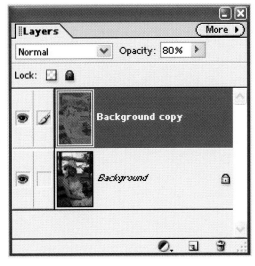

ABOUT THE UNDO HISTORY PALETTE

When you edit an image in Photoshop Elements, the application remembers the last 20 steps you've applied to the image. You can undo the last step by choosing **Edit I Undo**. You can move backward a step at a time by choosing **Edit I Step Backward**. When you step backward you momentarily erase the effects of that step. After stepping backward, you can move forward a step at a time by choosing **Edit I Step Forward**. You can also manually select a step from within the Undo palette. To access the Undo History palette shown in the following illustration, choose **Window I Undo Palette**, or click the **Undo Palette** in the Palette Docking area. In the Undo History palette, you can step backward and forward by clicking and dragging the right pointing arrow on the left side of the palette. You can delete a selected step and all steps that were applied after it by selecting the step and dragging it to the Trashcan icon near the bottom of the palette.

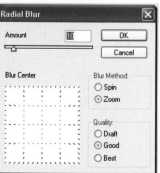

Create a Zoom Blur

One very cool effect photographers use is to mount a camera on a tripod and select a small aperture (high f-stop number) to achieve a slow shutter speed. Then they take a picture of an object with their zoom lens at its lowest magnification and quickly zoom to the highest magnification. The effect makes it look as though the object is rushing toward you. You can achieve the same effect in Photoshop Elements using the Radial Blur filter.

1. Open the image to which you want to apply the zoom blur effect. The following image shows a perfect candidate for this effect, a close-up of a hot rod. Unfortunately, the man at the side of the photo and the couple on the right distract viewers from the car.

2. Choose **Filter I Blur I Radial Blur** to open the dialog box shown to the right. Notice that this dialog box does not have a preview.

3. Drag the slider to the desired blur amount. A value between 10 and 15 works well for this effect.

4. In the Blur Method section, click the **Zoom** radio button.

ABOUT COREL PHOTO PAINT

If you like images that look like paintings, Corel has an application called Painter 9. The application features tools that work just like natural media paint brushes. If oil painting is your fancy, choose from one of the many oil brushes. When they're applied to an image, they look like dabs from an oil painter's brush. If you use the brushes in conjunction with the textured materials, you can simulate an oil on canvas look. But you're not limited to just oil paint. Corel Painter 9 has pastels, colored pencils, watercolor brushes, and so on.

Corel also has a feature that enables you to clone a photograph. You can use the natural media brushes to make the clone look like a painting. After you clone the photo, you select it and clear the canvas. You then enable Tracing Paper, which lets you use the natural media brushes as clones to trace over the areas of the original image. The end result is a photograph that looks like a painting. The natural media brushes work best with a digital tablet, but you can get an acceptable result by carefully controlling a mouse. This image was created using the previous version of the software, Corel Painter 8.

5. In the Quality section, click the desired quality radio button. Choose **Best** for the high quality image (at the expense of a longer render time).

6. Click **OK** to apply the effect. The following image shows the hot rod after the effect has been applied.

Simulate a Fish-Eye Lens

1. Open an image that you want to appear as though it was photographed with a fish-eye lens.

2. Select the **Crop** tool.

3. Click at the top of the image and, while holding down the SHIFT key, drag the tool to the bottom of the image. When you hold down the SHIFT key, you constrain the cropping box to a square, which is perfect for a fish-eye look.

4. Click the **Commit** button on the options bar (it looks like a check box). Alternatively, you can press ENTER or RETURN.

5. Select the **Elliptical Marquee** tool and create a circular section that stretches from top to bottom and side to side, as shown on the following page. Remember, to create a perfect circle, hold down the SHIFT key while dragging. Press the SPACEBAR momentarily to move the selection while creating it.

6. Choose **Filter | Distort | Spherize**.

7. Drag the Amount slider to 100, as shown to the right.

8. Click **OK** to apply the filter.

9. Choose **Select | Inverse**.

10. Choose **Edit | Fill** to open the Fill dialog box.

11. Click the down arrow to the right of the Use field and choose **Black** from the drop-down menu, as shown below.

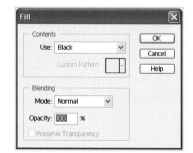

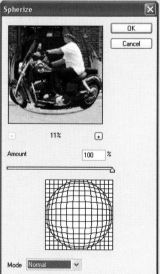

12. Click **OK** to fill the selection.

13. Choose **Select | Deselect**. The following image shows an image with this effect applied.

Chapter 9

Organizing Your Digital Image Library

When you start using your digital camera in earnest, you'll soon have many folders of images on your hard drive. If you followed the advice I presented in Chapter 7, your folders have logical names that make it easy for you to figure out what images are stored in what folder. In this chapter, you'll learn steps to further organize your digital image galleries and archive them to CD disc or an external hard drive.

Organize Your Digital Image Library

After several months of picture taking, your hard drive may have hundreds or thousands of images. If you employ good housekeeping and segregate similar image files into a named folder when you download them from your camera

TIP

You can also launch the File Browser by clicking the **File Browser** icon within Photoshop Elements.

to the computer, you've taken the first step in organizing your photos. The Photoshop Elements Browser is your biggest ally when it comes to organizing your digital image library.

Launch the File Browser

1. Launch Photoshop Elements.

2. Choose **Window I File Browser**. The following image shows the File Browser as launched within Photoshop Elements.

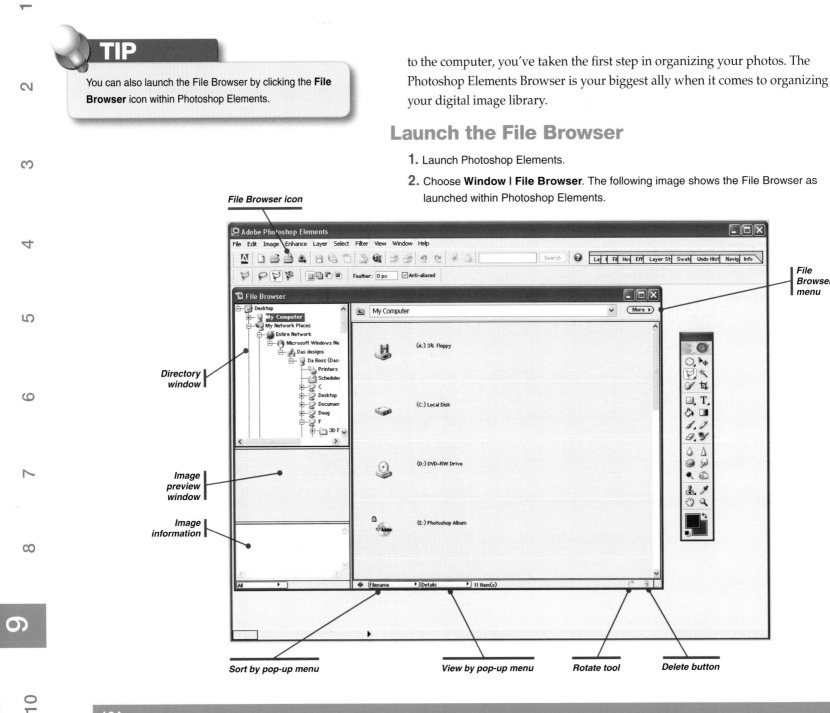

File Browser icon

File Browser menu

Directory window

Image preview window

Image information

Sort by pop-up menu

View by pop-up menu

Rotate tool

Delete button

Navigate to a Folder of Images

If you followed my suggestions from Chapter 7, you have a main folder for all of your digital images that is divided into subfolders that contain images: photographed at a certain place, of a particular subject or person, or at a certain time. The Photoshop Elements Browser defaults to the last folder you viewed. The following steps show how to navigate through the folders on your hard drive to view the desired folder.

1. Launch the File Browser.

2. In the Directory window, select your main image folder. After selecting your main image folder, the subfolders appear in the main window on the right side of the browser, as shown next.

TIP

You can resize the windows in the File Browser, by clicking and dragging the dividers.

TIP

You can move images into another folder by selecting their thumbnails in the browser window and dropping them into the desired folder.

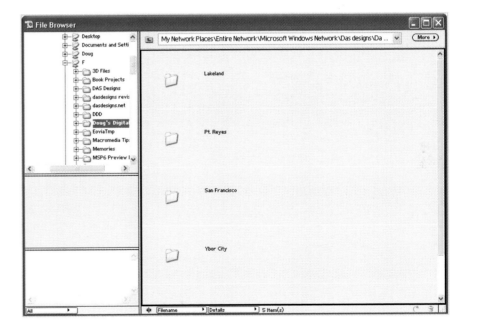

TIP

When managing images from within the File Browser, dock all palettes and maximize the File Browser to view more image thumbnails.

TIP

Click the **Toggle Expanded View** button to hide all windows except the thumbnails. This is the digital equivalent of a light box. Click the button again to display all browser windows.

3. Double-click a folder to display thumbnail versions of the images within the folder, as shown next.

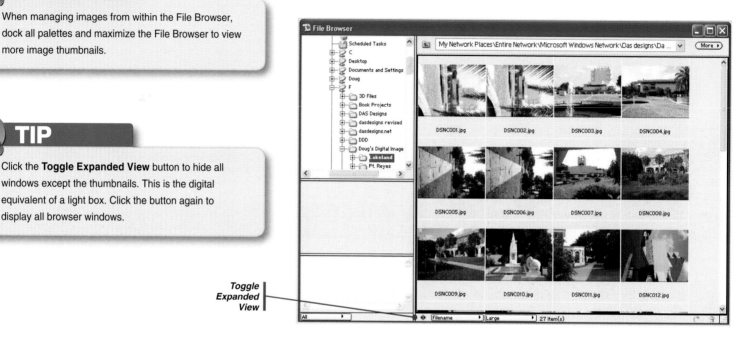

Toggle
Expanded
View

Work with Thumbnails

When you open the File Browser to a folder of images, they are displayed as they were when you last opened the File Browser. You can display images as small, medium, or large thumbnails, or you can display each image file as a thumbnail followed by pertinent details of the file. When you display a folder of images, you have the equivalent of a digital light box.

Change Thumbnail Size

You can change thumbnail size at any time. Changing thumbnail size enables you to view more thumbnails at one time when you select a small thumbnail size or more image details when you choose a larger thumbnail size.

1. Open an image folder.

2. Choose a thumbnail size from the View By drop-down menu shown next.

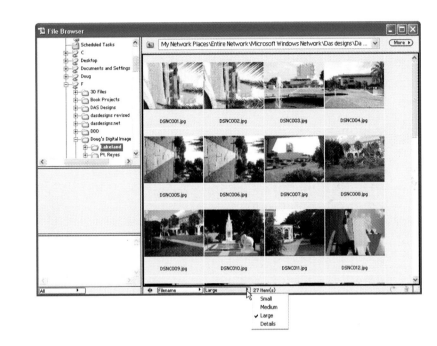

View Details

If you require more information than the thumbnail image offers, you can view a small thumbnail of a file and pertinent details about the image file. This option is handy when you need to know information, such as the file size, date created, or date modified, about a file before opening it.

1. Open an image folder.

2. Choose **Details** from the View By drop-down menu shown previously. The following image shows image files as viewed by the Details option.

QUICKFACTS

ABOUT THE FILE BROWSER MENU

In addition to using icons to perform tasks in the File Browser, you can also use the File Browser menu. The File Browser menu gives you a few additional commands. For example, you can rotate thumbnails 180 degrees. You can also use the Open command to open multiple files you have selected in the File Browser. To open the menu shown here, click the **More** button in the upper-right corner of the File Browser.

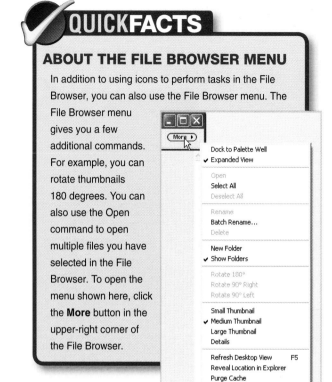

NOTE

After rotating the thumbnails, Photoshop Elements displays a dialog box telling you that only the thumbnails are rotated and that the images will be rotated the next time the files are opened in Photoshop Elements.

Rotate Images

If your camera does not have an option to rotate images, pictures that were photographed with a vertical composition will be displayed horizontally in the File Browser. You can rotate images as needed so that they display properly in the File Browser:

1. Open an image folder.

2. Select the image thumbnails that are not displayed properly. Click a thumbnail image to select it and then CTRL-click (Windows), or COMMAND-click (Macintosh), to select additional images you want to rotate.

3. Click the **Rotate** icon at the bottom of the File Browser to rotate selected images 90 degrees clockwise.

4. ALT-click (Windows) or OPTION-click (Macintosh) the **Rotate** icon at the bottom of the File Browser to rotate selected images 90 degrees counterclockwise, as shown next.

QUICKSTEPS

DELETING IMAGES

After you download images to your computer and view the thumbnails in the File Browser, you'll see some that are obvious candidates for deletion. You can easily delete one or more files from the File Browser.

1. Open an image folder.

2. View the files as large thumbnails so you'll be able to see shots that didn't turn out as planned. Double-click a file to open it in Photoshop Elements if you're in doubt as to whether you should delete a file or not.

3. Select the files you want to delete. Click the first file to select it and CTRL-click (Windows) or COMMAND-click (Macintosh) additional files you want to delete.

4. Click the **Delete** icon that looks like a trashcan. Photoshop Elements displays a dialog box asking you to confirm deletion, as shown next. Alternatively, you can drag the selected files to the Delete icon.

Adobe Photoshop Elements

Are you sure you want to send these 3 files to the recycle bin?

Yes   No

☐ Don't show again

5. Click **Yes** to delete the files.

TIP

To prevent the Confirm Deletion dialog box from appearing every time you want to delete files, click the **Don't Show Again** check box in the lower-left corner of the dialog box.

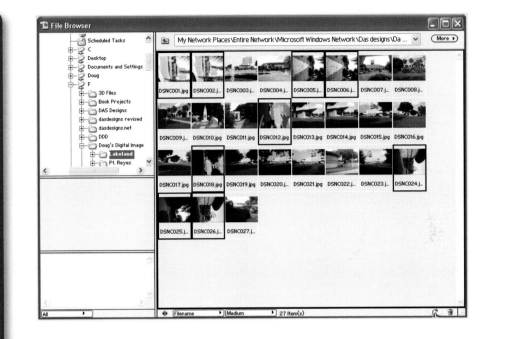

Sort Images

By default the File Browser sorts all images by filename. You can, however, change the parameter by which files are sorted. You can sort files by filename, width, height, file size, resolution, file type, date created, or date modified:

1. Open the desired file folder.

2. Choose the desired option for sorting files from the Sort By menu shown next.

RENAMING YOUR DIGITAL IMAGES

When you take a picture with your digital camera, the camera creates a filename for the image. The filename contains a prefix determined by the camera manufacturer, followed by a number. Unfortunately, the filename doesn't give you a clue about the image. You can use the File Browser to rename every digital image you own. For example, if you have a folder filled with JPEG images from your vacation to Disneyland, you can rename the files: Disney01.jpg, Disney02.jpg, and so on.

1. Launch Photoshop Elements and open the File Browser as outlined previously.

2. Navigate to the folder that contains the files you want to rename.

3. Select the files you want to rename by clicking their thumbnails. You can select contiguous files by SHIFT-clicking the first and last thumbnails of the files you want to rename, or you can select noncontiguous files by CTRL-clicking (Windows) or COMMAND-clicking (Macintosh) each file you want to select.

4. Click the **More** button in the upper-right corner of the File Browser, and from the drop-down menu choose **Batch Rename** to open the Batch Rename dialog box shown next.

Continued . . .

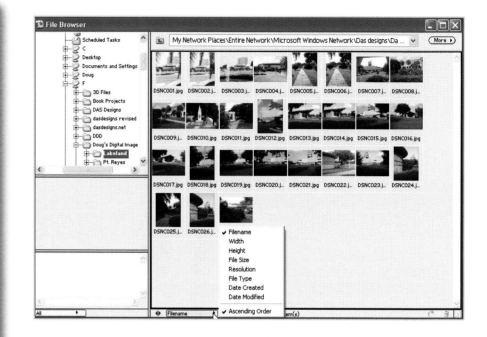

NOTE

You can also batch process files currently open in Photoshop Elements.

Batch Process Image Files

You use the Photoshop Elements Batch Processing command to convert files from one file type to another. This option is especially useful if you have a folder of high-resolution files that you want to resize and save in a different file format. When you batch process files, you can also rename the files, resize the files, specify a different destination folder, and so on.

1. Choose **File I Batch Processing** to open the dialog box shown on the following page (top-right illustration).

2. Select the desired option from the Files to Convert drop-down menu. The default option is Folder, which enables you to batch process all files in a folder.

RENAMING YOUR DIGITAL IMAGES
(Continued)

Batch Rename

Destination Folder
- ● Rename in same folder
- ○ Move to new folder

Browse...

File Naming

Example: Lakeland001.gif

| Lakeland | ▼ | + | 3 Digit Serial Number | ▼ |

Compatibility: ☑ Windows ☑ Mac OS 9 ☑ Unix

OK
Cancel

5. Accept the default option of storing renamed files in the same folder. Alternatively, you can click the **Move to New Folder** radio button, which enables the Browse button. Click the **Browse** button and then navigate to the folder where you want the renamed files stored.

6. Select the default naming option (Document Name) and type the name you want to replace it. For example, if you're renaming pictures of your wife, type your wife's first name.

Continued . . .

CAUTION

Do not enter a value for width or height that is larger than the dimensions of the files you are converting. When you enter a larger dimension, Photoshop Elements has to increase the size of pixels to the new image size at the current resolution and image degradation will result.

CAUTION

If you choose a higher resolution than the current resolution of the images you are processing, do not resize the images.

3. Click the **Source** button and navigate to the folder of files you want to process.

4. Click the **Include All Subfolders** check box if you want to process all files in subfolders of the selected folder.

5. Click the down arrow to the right of the Convert File Type field and choose an option from the drop-down menu shown here at bottom to the right.

6. If you want to resize the images, enter a value in the Width or Height text field and leave Constrain Proportions checked.

7. Click the down arrow from the right of the Resolution field and choose the desired resolution from the drop-down menu.

8. Click the **Rename Files** check box if you want to rename the files you are processing. Refer to the "Renaming Your Digital Images" sidebar for detailed instructions on these options.

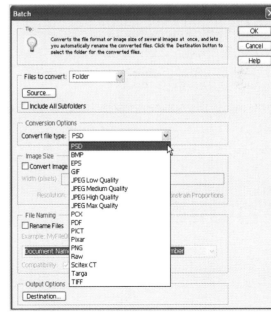

RENAMING YOUR DIGITAL IMAGES

(*Continued*)

7. Click the down arrow to the right of the next field and choose one of the following: 1 Digit Serial Number, 2 Digit Serial Number, 3 Digit Serial Number, or 4 Digit Serial number. There are other options available, but serial number is the logical choice when you're renaming several images and giving them the same name. After you choose your options, the example text updates to show you what the filename will look like after you rename the files.

8. By default, the File Browser renames the files so they're compatible with your operating system. If you're sharing the files with other people who own computers with different operating systems, choose one or both of the remaining options.

9. Click **OK** to rename the selected files.

TIP

Click the **Make New Folder** button to create a new folder in which to store the processed files.

NOTE

The example text shows the GIF file extension no matter what file format the images being renamed are in. Not to worry, Photoshop Elements will rename the files with the proper file extension.

NOTE

The remaining options will be operating systems other than the one installed on the computer from which you are renaming the files. Photoshop Elements can name files so that they are compatible with the following operating systems: Windows, Unix, or Mac OS9.

9. Click the **Destination** button if you want to save the files in a different folder. This opens the Browse for Folder dialog box shown here.

10. Navigate to the folder in which you want to store the files.

11. Click **OK** to close the Browse for Folder dialog box.

12. Click **OK** to process the selected files.

Archive Your Images

In a perfect world, computers would operate flawlessly and hard drives would last forever. Unfortunately neither event occurs. Computers will crash when you least expect them to, and if they crash hard, they're liable to corrupt some of your files. In this regard, you should always archive your digital images, and archive them frequently. That way if the worst-case scenario happens, you have backups of your digital images. CD discs are dirt cheap. Some people may think it's more logical to archive files to a DVD disc, but neither CDs nor DVDs are infallible. If a DVD disc is damaged, you lose almost 5GB of images. If a CD disc goes bad, you lose 700MB of images.

Create a Contact Sheet

When you've got hundreds of images stored on your hard drive, you use the File Browser to view a thumbnail image of the file before opening it. However, when you run low on hard disk space and save your files to CD discs before deleting them from the hard drive, you'll have to pop each disc in the CD drive and then search for the desired files with the File Browser—a tedious task at best. Fortunately, there is a better way. You can create a contact sheet for the images you store on CD discs. A contact sheet is a printed page that shows thumbnail-size pictures of image files. You can then store printed contact sheets in a loose-leaf binder for future reference.

1. Choose **File** I
   Print Layouts I
   Contact Sheet
   to open the dialog
   box shown here.

2. Click the **Browse**
   button to open the
   Browse for Folder
   dialog box.

3. Browse to the
   folder that
   contains the
   images for which
   you want to create
   a contact sheet.

```
Contact Sheet
  Source Folder
    [ Browse... ]  F:\Doug's Digital Image Library\Lakeland\          [ OK ]
    ☑ Include All Subfolders                                          [ Cancel ]
                                                                      [ Help ]
  Document
           Width: 8        inches    ▼
          Height: 10       inches    ▼
      Resolution: 72       pixels/inch ▼
            Mode: RGB Color           ▼
    ☑ Flatten All Layers
  Thumbnails
           Place: across first        ▼
         Columns: 4            Width:  1.98   inches
            Rows: 4           Height: 1.73   inches
    ☑ Use Filename As Caption
            Font: Arial          ▼    Font Size: 8 pt  ▼
```

4. Click the **Include
   All Subfolders** check box to add images in the subfolders to your contact sheet.

5. Type values in the Width and Height fields to specify the document size of the
   contact sheet.

6. Type a value in the Resolution field.

7. Click the down arrow to the right of the Mode field and choose **RGB Color**
   or **Grayscale** from the drop-down menu.

8. Accept the default Flatten All Layers option and Photoshop Elements will flatten the
   image before shrinking it to thumbnail size. This does not alter the original file in any
   way. I advise you to leave this option selected, as the resulting thumbnail file will be
   a smaller file size.

9. Click the down arrow to the right of the Place field and choose an option from the
   drop-down menu. This option determines how Photoshop Elements places the
   thumbnails in the finished document. Your options are Across First, which fills the
   contact sheet from right to left by rows, or Down First, which fills the contact sheet
   from top to bottom one column at a time.

10. Type values in the Columns and Rows fields. This determines how many thumbnails
    Photoshop Elements fits on a sheet. As you enter different values, the Width and
    Height information fields change to show you what size the resulting thumbnails
    will be.

TIP

If you're printing the contact sheet on 8-1/2 × 11 letter-size paper, accept the default 8 × 10 size.

TIP

The default resolution of 72 won't give you a very clear thumbnail. Specify a resolution of 150 and you'll get a contact sheet that is much easier to see.

TIP

To create an insert for a CD jewel case, select six images that represent the photos archived on a CD. Create a contact sheet 4-3/4–inches square. Print the contact sheet and trim it to fit the jewel case.

TIP

If you're creating a contact sheet for images with long filenames, type lower values in the Columns and Rows field to create bigger thumbnails and choose a smaller font size to display the entire filename below each contact sheet image.

QUICKSTEPS

CREATING FOLDERS FOR CD ARCHIVES

When you archive images to a CD disc, you can create a folder for each disc. If you create contact sheets for your image folders, you'll have a handy cross-reference.

1. Create a new folder.

2. Rename the folder. A logical naming sequence would be Images_001, Images_002, and so on.

3. Drag and drop the image folders you want to archive into the folder you just created.

TIP

While you're using your computer's operating system to add image folders to the archive folder, pay attention to the overall size of the folder. Make sure you don't exceed the available space available on the CD media to which you'll archive the files.

11. Accept the default Use Filename as Caption option. This option prints the filename below the thumbnail, which enables you to cross reference the thumbnail with the filename and select the proper image.

12. Click the down arrow to the right of the Font field and choose the desired font from the drop-down menu.

13. Click the down arrow to the right of the Font Size field and choose the desired option from the drop-down menu.

14. Click **OK**. Photoshop Elements resizes the images and creates the contact sheet. This process may take a considerable amount of time if you're creating contact sheets for a folder that contains a lot of images. Shown at right is an example of one-page contact sheet.

15. Choose **File | Save** to save the file in the desired format for future printing or future use. Alternatively, choose **File | Print** to print the contact sheet immediately and close the file without saving.

Archive Images to CD Discs

After you've created contact sheets and copied the image folders you want to archive into different folders, you're ready to archive the files to a CD disc. Windows and Macintosh operating systems both have built-in CD burning applications. Alternatively, you can purchase a third-party application such as Nero (Windows) or Toast (Macintosh).

Burning CD discs is processor intensive. To safeguard against a system crash, or corrupt data on a CD, exit all applications other than the one being used to burn the CD.

1. Open the file folder that contains the files you're going to archive to disc.

2. Insert a blank CD in a read/write CD drive. Your operating system recognizes the disc. If you're using a Windows-based computer, a dialog box opens offering you options. Select the option to open a writable folder. If you're using a Macintosh machine, a dialog box opens asking if you want to burn the disc.

3. Arrange the two windows side by side as shown next.

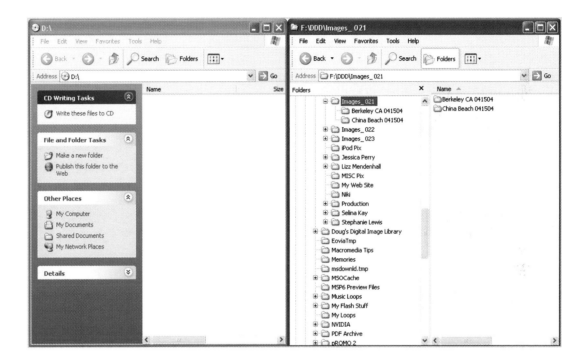

Don't use a regular marker to write on the CD disc. Regular markers can bleed through and damage your data. You can find CD- and DVD-safe markers at your local office supply store.

4. Drag and drop the files into the CD disc folder, as shown here.

5. Write the files to the CD.

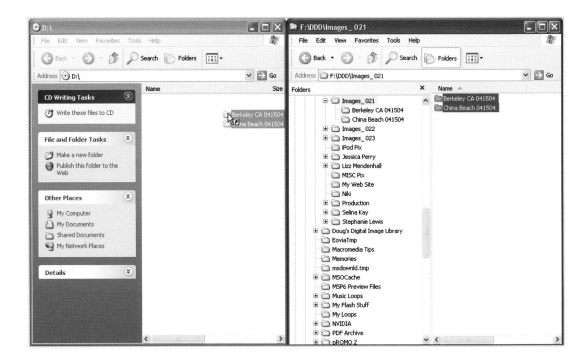

Back Up Image Files to an External Hard Drive

If you use your computer a lot, your hard drive takes a beating. Every time you launch a program or open a file, your computer's faithful servant the hard drive spins, locates, and serves up the required information. Like any mechanical device, a hard drive is subject to failure, and they will fail when you least expect it. If you're fortunate, you may be able to recover the data from the crashed hard drive. Rather than suffer the loss of your image gallery when a hard drive crashes, you can be proactive and back up your files to an external hard drive. You can purchase an external 80GB hard drive for as little as $150 at your local

computer retail outlet, which is cheap insurance compared to the loss of your prized digital images. Most external hard drives plug into an external AC adapter and connect to a computer USB or FireWire port. Some external hard drives have ports to connect to both USB and FireWire. After you connect the device to a USB or FireWire port, your computer recognizes the device and you can copy files to the hard drive. If you get in the habit of copying all updated folders to the device once a week, you'll always have a backup of your digital images and other important information.

How To...

- *Create a Picture Package*
- *Optimize and Resize the Image*
- *Send the Image via E-mail*
- *Optimize Images for the Web*
- *Create a Web Photo Gallery*
- *Import Images to Photoshop Album*
- *Create a Virtual Slide Show*
- *Create a Calendar*
- *Create a Video CD*
- *Create a Photo Album*
- *Create an eCard*
- *Print with Preview*
- *Choosing the Right Paper*
- *Use Online Printing Services*
- *Preserving Your Photos*
- *Create a Photo Book*
- *Investigating Alternative Papers*

Chapter 10

Sharing Your Digital Photographs

After editing your images, you're ready to share them with the world or a few close friends. With Photoshop Elements you can create pictures packages, optimize images for the Web, and create web photo galleries. In this chapter, I also cover Photoshop Elements' companion software, Photoshop Album. With this application you can create virtual slide shows, eCards, greeting cards, and more.

Share Your Digital Images

There are so many ways you can share digital images with friends and family. You can create a picture package in Photoshop Elements that combines several sizes of the same image on one sheet of paper. If you know a bit about web design, you can optimize photographs for use on a website. If you own the companion software to Photoshop Elements, Photoshop Album, you can create photo albums, greeting cards, virtual slide shows, and much more.

Create a Picture Package

When you create a picture package in Photoshop Elements, you can choose from several different layout options. For example, you can create a picture package that combines two 5 × 7 photographs on a single page or a picture package that combines one 5 × 7 and two 3 × 5 photographs on a single page. After you choose the layout, Photoshop Elements does its magic and creates the picture package, which you can then print out.

1. Open the image for which you want to create a picture package.

2. Choose **File | Print Layouts | Picture Package** to open the dialog box shown next. The default picture package prints two 5 × 7 images on an 8 × 10 sheet.

3. Accept the default page size (8 × 10), or click the down arrow to the right of the field and choose a different size from the drop-down menu.

4. Click the down arrow to the right of the Layout field and choose an option from the drop-down menu shown to the left.

TIP

You can also create a picture package for every image in a folder by choosing Folder from the Use drop-down menu.

CAUTION

Do not specify a resolution that is higher than the resolution of the original image.

TIP

If you want to create a Grayscale Picture Package, you're better off converting the image to grayscale using the technique covered in the "Convert an Image to Grayscale" section of Chapter 8. This will produce an RGB image that looks like a black and white photograph. Choose the default RGB Color mode to create a picture package that will give you more pleasing results.

5. Type a value in the Resolution field. If you're creating a picture package to be printed, specify a resolution of at least 200ppi (pixels per inch), preferably 300ppi if your printer will support it. Anything less will produce unacceptable results.

6. Click the down arrow to the right of the Mode field and choose the desired option from the drop-down menu. Your choices are RGB Color or Grayscale.

7. Accept the default Flatten All Layers option. I recommend you accept this option as it causes Photoshop Elements to flatten all layers in the image, resulting in a smaller file size. Your original image will be unaltered.

8. Click the down arrow to the right of the Content field in the Label area if you want to add a label to the image. This reveals the drop-down menu shown next.

9. If you choose one of the Label options, specify the Font, Font Size, Color, Opacity, and Position as shown here.

10. Click **OK** to create the picture package. The following image shows a completed picture package.

Label	
Content:	Custom Text
Custom Text:	Cover Girl
Font:	Arial
Font Size:	12 pt
Color:	Black
Position:	Centered
Rotate:	None

Opacity: 100 %

11. Choose **File I Save** to save the picture package for future use.

12. Choose **File I Print** to open the Print dialog box shown next.

Print

Printer
Name: EPSON Stylus Photo 925   Properties...
Status: Ready
Type: EPSON Stylus Photo 925
Where: USB001
Comment: ☐ Print to file

Print range
● All
○ Pages from: to:
○ Selection

Copies
Number of copies: 1

☑ Collate

OK   Cancel

13. Click the down arrow to the right of the Name field and choose the desired printer.

14. Click **Properties** to open the Properties dialog box for the selected printer. This dialog box enables you to choose the paper size to fit the media on which you are going to print the picture

package. The image at right shows the Properties dialog box for an Epson Stylus Photo 925 printer. The dialog box varies depending on the printer you choose. Refer to your printer user manual for specific instructions on selecting paper, layout, and other parameters that apply to your printer.

Send an Image via E-mail

After editing an image, you can send it to a friend via e-mail. However, if you're working with a large image that has a high resolution, you'll have to cut it down to size before sending it, or the file will take too long to download.

Optimize and Resize the Image

If you want to share a high-resolution photo with a friend via e-mail, your best bet is to save a scaled-down version of the file in the JPEG format:

1. Open the image you want to e-mail.

2. Choose **Image | Resize | Image Size** to open the Image Size dialog box.

3. Resize the image so that the largest dimension is 640 pixels or less and resample the image to 72ppi, the resolution of a computer monitor. Shown at right is an image being resized for e-mail delivery.

4. Choose **File | Save As** to open the Save As dialog box.

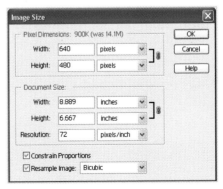

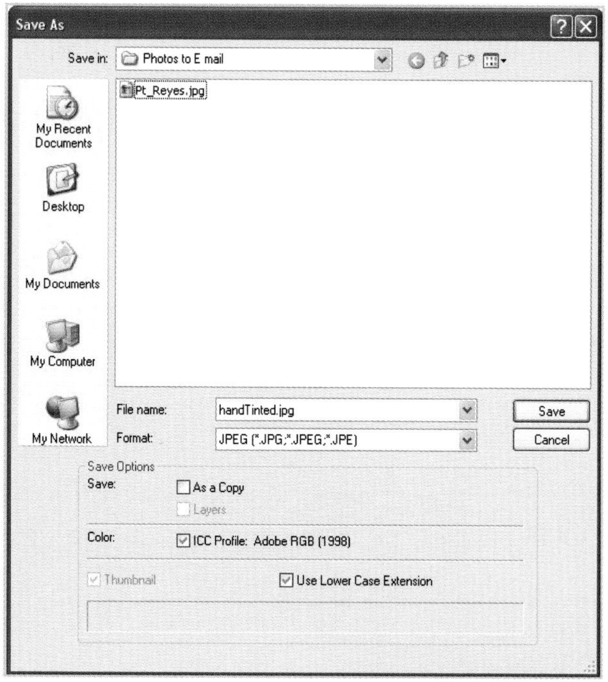

TIP

If you know the Internet connection speed of the recipient to whom you are sending the picture, click the down arrow to the right of the default 56.6Kbps setting and choose the desired setting from the drop-down menu. This updates the download time to your recipient's connection speed.

TIP

To open a recently saved file, choose **File | Open Recent** and choose the file from the Recently Saved Files drop-down list, which contains the last 10 files you saved.

5. Choose **JPEG** from the Format drop-down menu shown above.

6. Click **Save**. The JPEG options dialog box opens.

7. Drag the Quality Slider to the left to reduce the image quality and the file size. Notice that the file size and download time is displayed in the Size section.

8. Click **OK** to save the file.

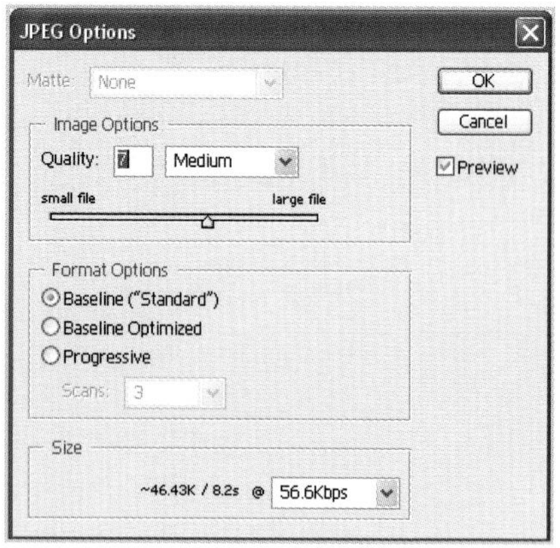

Send the Image via E-mail

1. Open the file you just optimized for e-mail delivery.

2. Choose **File | Attach to E-mail**. Photoshop Elements launches your default e-mail application; the image is already attached, as shown next.

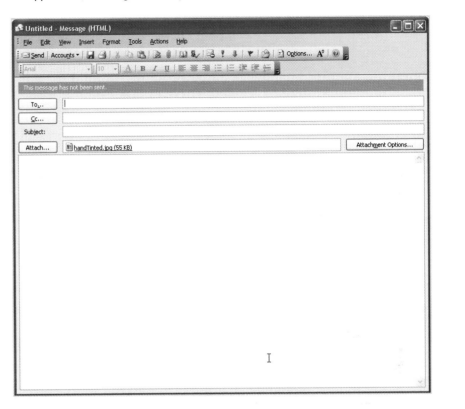

3. Choose your recipients, fill in the subject matter, and add your message to the e-mail.

4. Send the e-mail.

Display Your Images at a Website

Many Internet Service Providers offer free websites to their customers, while others offer web hosting services at discounted prices. Today it's easier than ever to create your own website. Your Internet Service Provider may even provide you with ready-built templates for creating a website. The following sections show how to optimize images for web viewing, and how to create a web photo gallery.

Optimize Images for the Web

There are two image file formats commonly used for images displayed on websites: GIF and JPEG. The GIF format is 8-bit color depth (256 colors) and is suitable only for images with areas of large color. Digital photographers who display images on the Web almost always use the JPEG format, which supports millions of colors. JPEG is known as a lossy image format because image data is lost when the file is compressed. The trick is to apply the correct amount of compression to achieve the best quality image and the smallest possible file size.

1. Open the image you want to optimize for the Web.

2. Choose **Image | Resize** to open the Image Size dialog box.

3. Resize the image to the desired size, and specify 72 for the resolution, as outlined previously in the "Optimize and Resize the Image" section of this chapter.

4. Choose **File | Save for Web** to open the dialog box shown on the following page.

5. Click the down arrow to the right of the Settings field, and choose a setting from the drop-down menu shown here. For a digital photograph, choose one of the JPEG settings.

6. Compare the compressed image in the right window with the original image in the left window. Note that the file size of the original image is noted below the left window, and the file size and download time is listed in the right window.

7. If the compressed image quality, file size, and download time are acceptable, click **OK**. If not, choose a different setting.

8. After clicking OK, the Save Optimized As dialog box opens, as shown to the left.

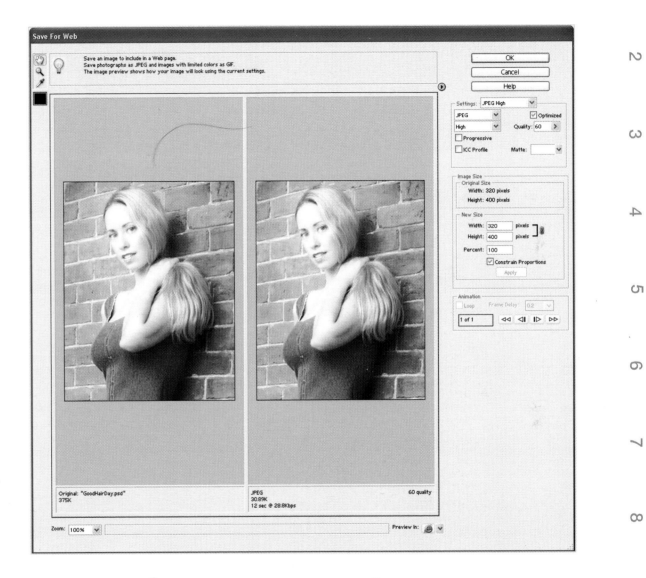

9. Accept the default filename or enter a new filename.

10. Navigate to the folder in which you want to store the file and then click **OK**.

Create a Web Photo Gallery

If you're not a web design guru, you can use Photoshop Elements to create a web photo gallery. The web photo gallery features neatly arranged thumbnails of the images you want to display. When clicked, the thumbnail reveals a full-size image. Now, how cool is that?

1. Choose **File | Create Web Photo Gallery** to open the dialog box shown here.

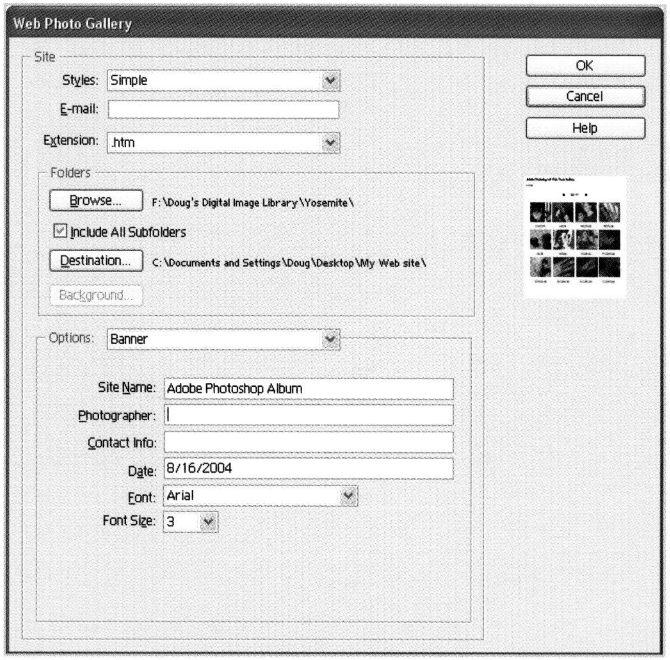

2. Click the down arrow to the right of the Styles menu and choose an option from the drop-down list. This list shows the different styles you can choose for your web photo gallery. Choose a style and the preview on the right side of the dialog box changes, as shown next.

TIP

Enter your e-mail address in the e-mail field to display it on your web photo gallery.

Web Photo Gallery

Site

Styles: Vertical Frame

E-mail:

Extension: .htm

Folders

Browse... F:\Doug's Digital Image Library \Yosemite\

☑ Include All Subfolders

Destination... C:\Documents and Settings\Doug\Desktop\My Web site\

Background...

Options: Banner

Site Name: Adobe Photoshop Album

Photographer:

Contact Info:

Date: 8/16/2004

Font: Arial

Font Size: 3

OK
Cancel
Help

TIP

Use the Create New Folder button to store your photo gallery and assorted files in a new folder.

3. Click the **Browse** button and then navigate to the folder that contains the images you want to display in your web photo gallery.

4. Click the **Destination** button to open the Browse for Folder dialog box.

5. Navigate to the folder in which you want to store your web photo gallery.

6. Click the down arrow to the right of the Options field to reveal the drop-down menu shown at right. These options let you specify what the web page banner looks like, the size of the large images, the size of the thumbnail images, custom colors for the background of the page, and security. The options are fairly self-explanatory, with the exception of the Large option, which will be discussed in the upcoming steps. If you run into a snag, click the **Help** button in the upper-right corner of the dialog box.

Banner
Large Images
Thumbnails
Custom Colors
Security

CAUTION

If you choose Custom, I advise you not to exceed 480 pixels for the Resize Images field.

7. Click the down arrow to the right of the Options field and choose **Large Images**. The Web Photo Gallery dialog box is reconfigured, as shown here.

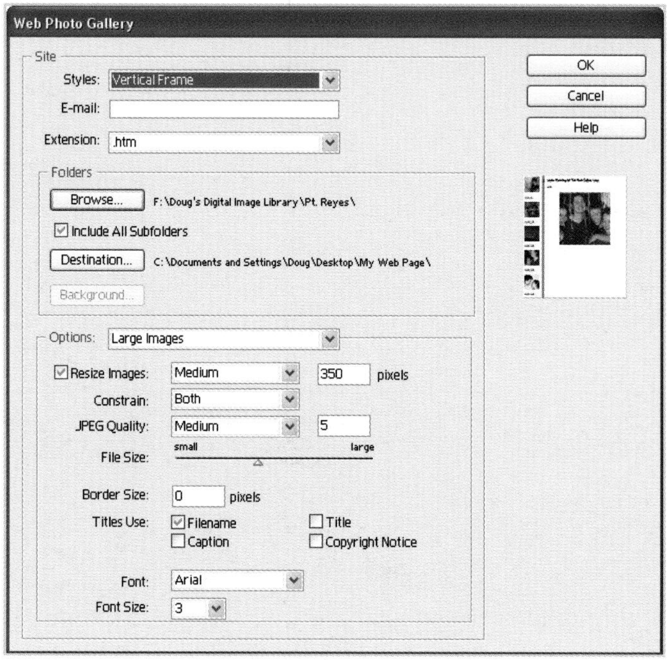

8. Accept the Resize Images option. This default option instructs Photoshop Elements to resize the images. If you don't want Photoshop Elements to resize the images, deselect the Resize Images check box.
9. Click the down arrow to the right of the Resize Images field and choose an option from the drop-down menu. This setting tells Photoshop Elements how wide to size the images. Your choices are Small (250 pixels), Medium (350 pixels), Large (450 pixels), or Custom. If you choose Custom, you can type the desired value in the text field. If your images are landscape, this option determines the width; if they are portrait, this option determines the height.
10. Accept the default Constrain option of Both as this proportionately resizes your images.

11. Click the down arrow to the right of the JPEG Quality field and choose an option from the drop-down menu. Alternatively, you can enter a value between 0 (for a low quality image, quick download) and 12 (for a high quality image, slow download). The default setting of 5 works well in most cases. Only choose a higher quality if your intended audience will access your website with a fast dial-up or broadband connection.

12. After setting the options for your web photo gallery, click **OK**. The following image shows a completed web photo gallery.

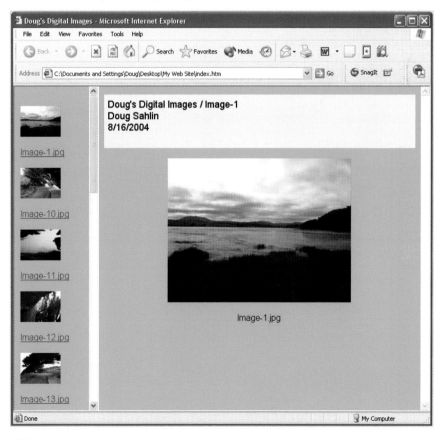

NOTE

When you create a web photo gallery, Photoshop Elements creates folders for pages, thumbnails, and images. These folders must be uploaded to the server in the same order they appear on your hard drive, otherwise you'll have broken links or missing images when the pages are displayed.

13. Upload the files to your web host server. For detailed instructions on uploading your web photo gallery, contact your web hosting service.

Share Your Digital Images with Photoshop Album

You may already own Photoshop Album, the feature-filled companion to Photoshop Elements. The next sections show you how to use the application to create a virtual slide show, a calendar, a video CD, a greeting card, and an eCard. If you don't already own Photoshop Album, you can purchase it from most retail outlets that sell computer software. As of this writing, Photoshop Album sells for $49.95.

Import Images to Photoshop Album

You create catalogs of images within Photoshop Album. You use images from these catalogs to create items such as slide shows, calendars, eCards, and so on. You can import images from your digital camera, a card reader, a scanner, or a folder of images. I'll cover importing images from a folder in this section.

1. Launch Photoshop Album. After you launch the application, the Photoshop Album Quick Guide, shown next, appears, giving you the option of viewing a tutorial by clicking one of the icons, or performing a task by clicking the applicable tab.

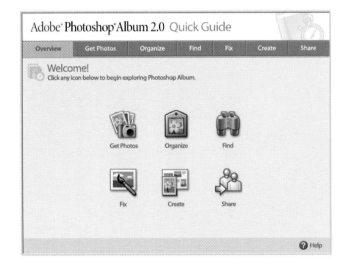

TIP

You can download a starter version of Photoshop Album from Adobe's website. This free version of the software doesn't contain all the functionality of the retail version, but it will give you an idea of what you can do with the application. The starter version runs indefinitely and can be downloaded from: http://www.adobe.com/products/photoshopalbum/starter.html.

TIP

You can prevent the Quick Guide from appearing when you launch the application by deselecting the Show On Start Up option in the lower-right corner of the Quick Guide.

2. Close the Quick Guide.

3. Click the **Get Photos** icon and choose **From Files and Folders** from the drop-down menu shown next.

NOTE

Importing images from a camera, card reader, or scanner requires that you have such a device connected to your computer. After selecting one of these import options, a menu-driven wizard guides you through the import process.

4. From the Get Photos from Files and Folders dialog box, navigate to the folder that contains the image files you want to import, as shown next.

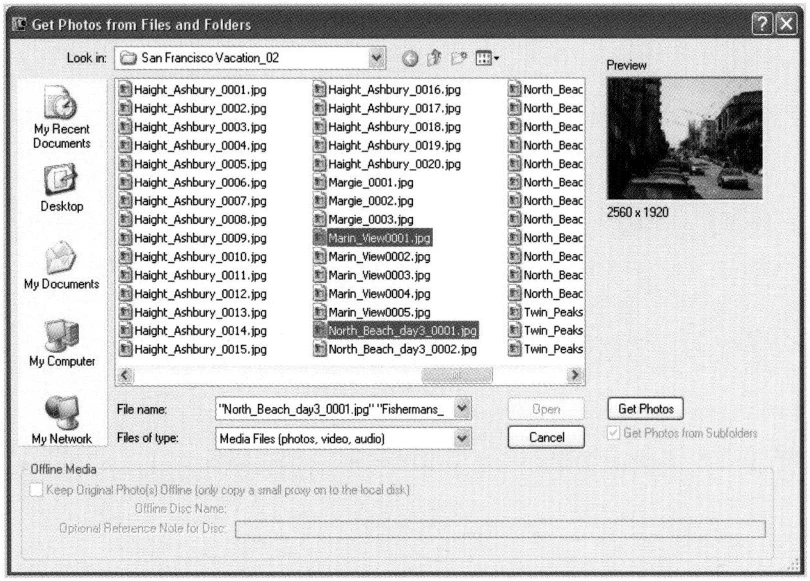

5. Select the files you want to import. You can select a range of images by selecting an image file and then SHIFT-clicking the last image file you want to import. You can import noncontiguous files by CTRL-clicking (Windows) or COMMAND-clicking (Macintosh) the files you want to import.

6. Click **Get Photos** to import the files into Photoshop Album. The following image shows Photoshop Album after several images have been imported.

NOTE

After you import files into Photoshop Album, only the recently imported files are shown. To show the entire catalog of all images you've imported, click **Show All**.

Create a Virtual Slide Show

You can use Photoshop Album to create a virtual slide show. The results can be
viewed by anyone who has the free Acrobat Reader installed on their computer.
You can choose from many different styles, add background music to the slide
show, and more.

1. Choose **Creations | Slide Show** to open the Creations Wizard, shown on the
   following page.

Choose Your Slideshow Style
Step: 1 **2** 3 4 5 6

Choose your Slideshow style:

Fall

Winter

Party

Fun for Kids

Everyday

Other Style

Travel

Travel
The perfect way to tell the story of your vacation.

Set up Your Slideshow
Step: 1 2 **3** 4 5 6

Include Title Page
☑ Title: Doug's Digtal Images

Body Pages
Photos Per Page: 1 ☑ Include Captions

Presentation Options
Background Music: SanFrancisco.wav Browse...
☑ Play Audio Captions
Transition: Fade Page Duration: 6 sec
☑ Include Play Controls ☐ Pause on Start / Manual Advance ☐ Allow Video to Resize
☑ Start Slideshow Automatically ☐ Repeat Slideshow

💡 Captions will not appear on the Title page. Read more about adding captions in Help.

2. Choose the desired slide show style and click **Next** to display the next page of the wizard, as shown in the illustration to the left.

3. If you accept the default title page option, type a title in the Title field. This option includes a title page using the first image in your slide show, and your desired title.

4. Click the **Photos Per Page** field and choose an option from the drop-down menu.

5. Click the **Include Captions** check box to deselect the default captions option. If you accept this option, Photoshop Album displays your photo caption underneath the photo as the slide show plays.

6. To add background music to your slide show, click the down arrow to the right of the Background Music field and choose a selection from the drop-down list. Alternatively, click the **Browse** button to the right of the Background Music field, navigate to the folder in which you store audio files, and then select the file you want to use as background music.

10

7. Deselect the default **Play Audio Captions** option and the slide show will not play any audio captions you've created for images.

8. Click the down arrow to the right of the current Transition option and choose the desired transition from the drop-down menu. This option determines how one image will transition into the next. For example, you can fade one image into the next, or dissolve one image into the next, and so on.

9. Click the down arrow to the right of the Page Duration field, and choose an option from the drop-down menu. This determines how long each image is displayed. Your options are 2, 4, or 10 seconds. Alternatively, you can select the current duration and type a different value.

10. Deselect the default **Include Play Controls** to create a slide show without play controls.

11. Deselect the default **Start Slideshow Automatically** option and the slide show will open in Adobe Reader or the full version of Acrobat. The user can then decide whether to view the slide show a page at a time or switch to full-screen mode and let the slide show advance automatically.

12. Select the **Pause on Start/Manual Advance** option to enable the viewer to advance the slide show using the play controls.

13. Select the **Repeat Slideshow** option and the slide show will loop back to the first slide when the slide show is over and then repeat the slide show.

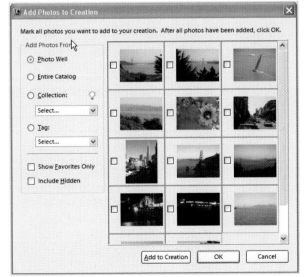

14. Select the **Allow Video to Resize** option to resize the slide show to the template window. Note that this will decrease image quality and slow down playback.

15. Click **Next** to open the Pick Your Pictures page of the wizard.

16. Click the **Add Photos** button to open the Add Photos to Creation dialog box, shown to the left.

17. Select the photos to add to the slide show and then click **OK** to add the photos.

18. Click **Next** to advance to the Customize Your Slideshow page.

Creations Wizard

Customize Your Slideshow

Step: 1 2 3 4 **5** 6

Doug's Digtal Images

Layout: Default   Title   Reset Photos

Full Screen Preview   < Back   Next >   Cancel

NOTE

After publishing a creation, it is added to the Photo Well. From the Photo Well you can preview the creation, edit the creation, republish the creation, and more. Right-click (Windows) or CONTROL-click (Macintosh) a creation to access a context menu of commands pertaining to your creation.

Creations Wizard - Doug's Digtal Images

Publish Your Slideshow

Step: 1 2 3 4 5 **6**

Summary

Output Options

Use the following options to view and share your creation:

Save as PDF...

Print...

E-mail...

Burn...

Order Online...

The creation will now be saved and will appear in the photo well, dated 8/17/2004. You may need to click the Show All button to see it.

Name: Doug's Digtal Images

☑ Use Title for Name

< Back   Done   Cancel

---

19. In the Customize Your Slideshow page, you can preview the slide show by clicking the control buttons at the bottom of the dialog box, as shown above. When you advance past the Title page, the Layout option become available, enabling you to change the number of images displayed on a page.

20. Click **Next** to advance to the Publish Your Slideshow page, shown to the left.

21. Choose the desired publishing option by clicking the applicable button on the right side of the dialog box. You can publish your slide show as a PDF document or e-mail the slide show. The image on the following page shows a page from a PDF slide show.

22. After publishing the application, click **Done**.

Create a Calendar

You can also use Photoshop Album to create a custom calendar with your digital pictures. You can choose from many different layouts. After creating your calendar, you can print it to share with friends and relatives.

1. Choose **Creations** | **Calendar** to launch the Creations Wizard, shown at the top of the following page.

2. Choose a calendar style and then click **Next** to advance to the Set Up Your Calendar page.

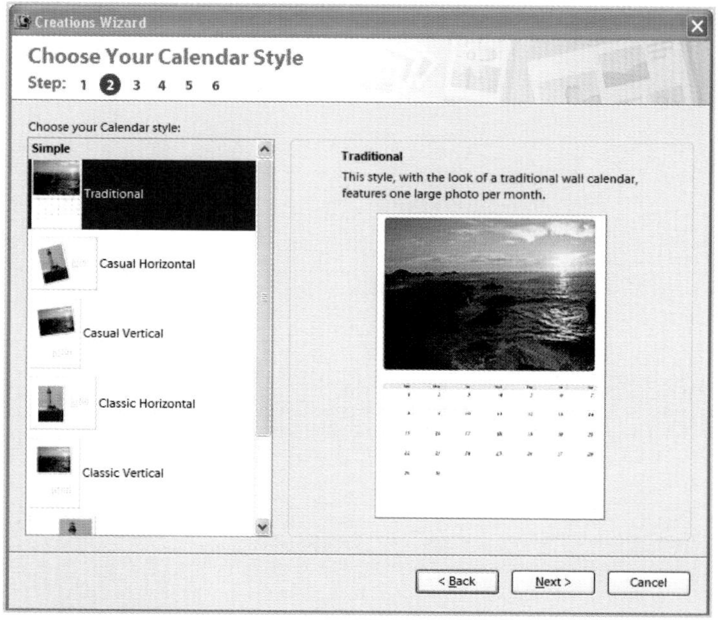

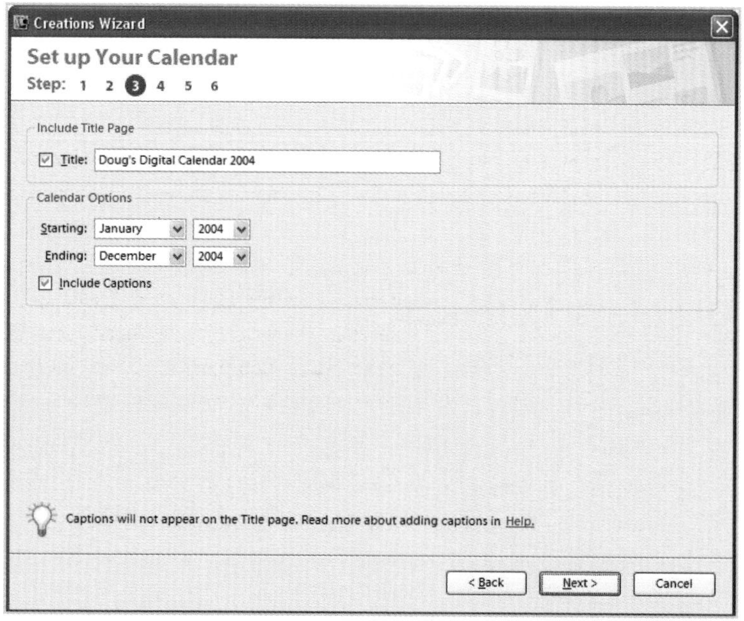

3. Type a title for the calendar, and from the drop-down lists, choose the calendar starting and ending dates, as shown at left.

4. Click **Next** to advance to the Pick Your Photos page.

5. Pick the photos you want to include with the calendar using the steps outlined previously in the "Create a Virtual Slide Show" section of this chapter. If you include a title page, remember to pick one more image than the number of months on your calendar.

6. Click **Next** to open the Customize Your Calendar page, shown on the following page (top illustration). From within this page you can preview each month of the calendar. If you don't like the way a photo looks on a page, click the **Back** button and pick a different photo for that month.

7. After previewing the calendar, click **Next** to open the Publish Your Calendar page, shown to the left.

8. Choose the desired publishing option by clicking the applicable button on the right side of the dialog box. You can publish your calendar as a PDF document, print the calendar, or e-mail the calendar. Each publishing option has different parameters. The image on the next page shows a page from a PDF calendar.

April
2005

Sun	Mon	Tue	Wed	Thu	Fri	Sat
					1	2
3	4	5	6	7	8	9
10	11	12	13	14	15	16
17	18	19	20	21	22	23
24	25	26	27	28	29	30

Create a Video CD

If you own a DVD player that will play CD-RWs, you can create a video
CD of your images and watch them on your television screen. You can add
background music to your video CD and specify how the images are displayed
on screen.

1. Choose **Creations I Video CD** to open the Choose Your Video CD Style page, shown
   next.

NOTE

If you don't choose High Quality on the Set Up Your Video CD page, you may be disappointed with the end result since Photoshop Album compresses the images to compensate for transitions, and if added, background music.

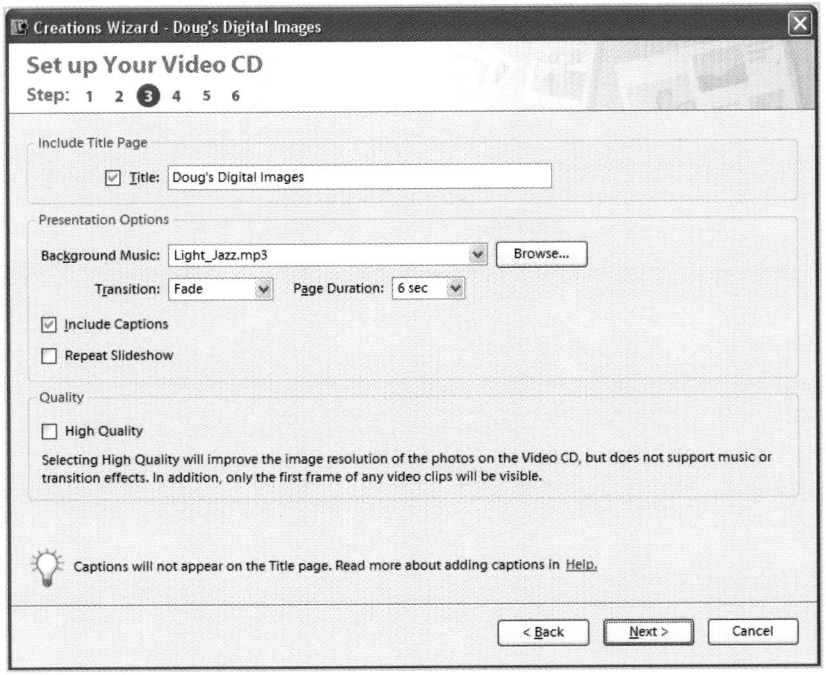

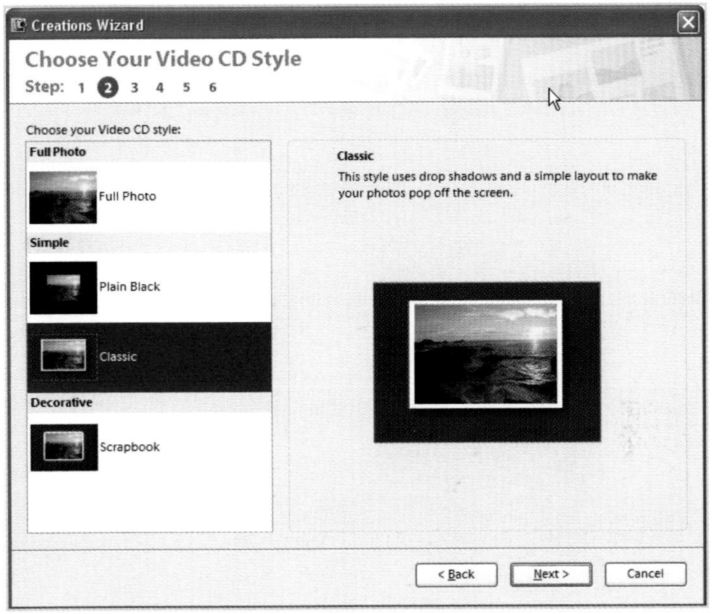

2. Choose the desired style and then click **Next** to open the Set Up Your Video CD page.

3. Type a title for the video CD and choose background music if desired, as shown to the left.

4. Choose the desired transition type from the Transition drop-down menu and specify the duration each image will be displayed.

5. Deselect the default Include Captions option to display the images without captions you have created for the images.

6. Click the **Repeat Slideshow** check box to repeat the slide show after it has finished.

7. Click the **High Quality** check box to increase the quality of the images on your video CD. Note that if you choose this option, your video CD will have no transitions between images and will not play background music.

8. Click **Next** to open the Pick Your Photos page.

9. Pick the photos to include on the video CD as outlined previously in the "Create a Virtual Slide Show" section of this chapter.

10. Click **Next** to display the Customize Your Video CD page. From within this page, you can preview each image in your video CD using the controls at the bottom of the dialog box.

11. Click **Next** after previewing the video CD to display the Publish Your Video CD page, shown next.

12. Insert a blank CD-RW in your CD drive.

13. Click the **Burn** button. The Burn dialog box appears, as shown to the left.

14. Choose your video format. National Television System Committee (NTSC) is the television video standard in the Americas and some Asian countries, while Phase Attenuating Line (PAL) is the standard for television video in most of the rest of the world.

15. Accept the default burn speed (half the maximum speed of your CD burner), or choose a different speed from the drop-down menu.

16. Click **OK** to burn the video CD. This may take some time depending on the speed of your CD burner and the number of images in your video CD.

Create a Photo Album

You can also create a photo album using images you've imported into Photoshop Album. When you create a photo album, you specify the number of images on each page and the style of album.

1. Choose **Creations | Photo Album** to launch the Choose Your Album Style page, shown here.

2. Choose the desired style and then click **Next** to display the Set Up Your Album page.

3. Type a title for your album and choose the number of images to display per page. If desired, include a header and/or footer by clicking the applicable check box and then typing the desired header and/or footer text, as shown on the next page.

Creations Wizard

Set up Your Album
Step: 1 2 **3** 4 5 6

Include Title Page

☑ Title: [   ]

Body Pages

Photos Per Page: [1   ▼] ☑ Include Captions ☑ Include Page Numbers

☐ Header: [   ]

☐ Footer: [   ]

Captions will not appear on the Title page. Read more about adding captions in Help.

[< Back] [Next >] [Cancel]

> **TIP**
>
> If your printer supports it, consider printing an album on high-quality scrapbook photo paper. This paper produces high-quality images. Remember to use a fixative to protect the images.

4. Click **Next** to open the Pick Your Photos page.

5. Pick the photos to include in your album as outlined previously in the "Create a Virtual Slide Show" section of this chapter.

6. Click **Next** to open the Customize Your Album page. From within this page, you can preview the album page by page. You can also change the number of images displayed on a given page.

7. Click **Next** after customizing your album to display the Publish Your Creation page.

8. Click the **Print** button to print your photo album.

Create a Greeting Card

You can use Photoshop Album to create a custom greeting card that will stand out from the store-bought variety. Your greeting card prints as a single-page document, which you fold in half and then fold in half again.

1. Choose **Creations | Greeting Card** to open the Choose Your Greeting Card Style page, shown next.

2. Choose the desired style and then click **Next** to open the Set Up Your Greeting Card page.

3. Type the desired title, greeting, and message as shown to the left.

4. Click **Next** to reveal the Pick Your Photos page.

5. Pick the photos to include in your album as outlined previously in the "Create a Virtual Slide Show" section of this chapter.

6. Click **Next** to open the Customize Your Greeting Card page. From within this page, you can resize the image and preview your greeting card.

7. Click **Next** to open the Publish Your Creation page.

8. Click the **Print** button and follow the prompts to print your greeting card on the desired printer.

9. Fold your greeting card.

10

Create an eCard

In Photoshop Album, you can create the digital equivalent of a greeting card, an eCard. An eCard is a PDF document that is attached to an e-mail. The recipient can view the eCard using the Adobe Reader. If the recipient doesn't have the Adobe Reader installed on their computer, the e-mail has a link to the Adobe web page where the Adobe Reader can be downloaded for free.

1. Choose **Creations I eCard** to open the Choose Your eCard Style page, shown next.

2. Choose the desired style and click **Next** to reveal the Set Up Your eCard page.

3. Type a title, greeting, message, and signature. You can also add background music to an eCard by selecting a preset from the Background Music drop-down menu, or clicking the Browse button and choosing a music selection stored on your computer.

4. Specify the transition type, page duration, and whether or not to include play controls, as shown in the following illustration.

CAUTION

Refrain from adding music to an eCard if your intended recipient accesses the Internet with a dial-up modem because the background music increases the file size, resulting in a lengthy download.

5. Click **Next** to display the Pick Your Photos page.

6. Pick the photos to include in your album as outlined previously in the "Create a Virtual Slide Show" section of this chapter.

7. Click **Next** to open the Customize Your eCard page. From within this page, you can preview your eCard.

8. Click **Next** to display the Publish Your eCard page.

9. Click the **E-mail** button to display Attach Creation Items to E-mail page, shown next.

10. Select a recipient from your contacts list.

11. To add a recipient to your contacts list, click the **Add Recipient** button to open the Add a Recipient dialog box.

12. Enter the recipient information as shown here, and click **OK** to add the recipient to your contacts list.

13. Accept the default filename for the attachment, or type a new one.

14. Choose the desired Size and Quality setting and then click **OK**. Photoshop Album publishes the eCard as a PDF document and launches your default e-mail application with the eCard as an attachment.

15. Send the e-mail.

Print Your Digital Photos

It's wonderful to edit your digital photos in Photoshop Elements and share them electronically with friends via e-mail and your website. However, nothing quite matches the thrill of being able to look at a printed image suitable for framing. If you own a photo-quality printer as discussed in Chapter 1, you can print hard copies of your digital pictures. In the sections that follow, you'll learn how to print your images from Photoshop Elements, choose the right paper, and seal your photographs so they stand the test of time.

Print with Preview

There's an old saying that what you see is what you get. The Photoshop Elements design team give credence to this wisdom, as they've included a Print Preview command. When you use this command, you can resize and reposition the photo relative to the media on which you are printing the image.

1. Open the image you want to print.

2. Choose **File | Print Preview** to open the Print Preview dialog box as shown in the following illustration.

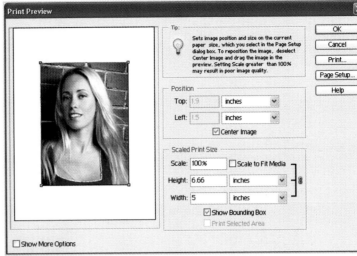

TIP

You can type a value in the Scale field to resize the image. For example, a value of 110% will increase the size of the image by 10 percent.

3. Click the **Page Setup** button to select the paper size, source, and orientation.

4. Deselect the Center Image check box if you want to manually position the image within the media. After deselecting this option, you can type values for the top and left position of the image or click inside the image and drag it to the desired position.

5. Click and drag a corner handle to resize the image within the media. Alternatively, you type a value in the Width or Height field to resize the image proportionately.

6. Click the **Show More Options** check box to reveal the printing options shown in the image at left.

7. Click the **Background** button to reveal the Adobe Color Picker, shown on the following page.

Color Picker

Select background color:

OK
Cancel
Help

○ H: 0 °
○ S: 0 %
○ B: 100 %
○ R: 255
○ G: 255
○ B: 255

☐ Only Web Colors   # FFFFFF

8. Drag the Color slider to select the desired hue, and then click and drag inside the Color field to select the desired saturation.

9. Click **OK** to exit the Color Picker.

10. Click the **Corner Crop Marks** check box to add crop marks around the image. This option creates useful guides that can be used to cut the photo to size with a paper trimmer.

11. Click **OK** to print the image.

Use Online Printing Services

If you don't own a photo-quality printer, you can still have photographic quality prints made of your digital images. Adobe Photoshop Elements and Adobe Photoshop Album have links within the software that enable you to order prints through third-party online services. After agreeing to the terms of service, you upload your images to the online service and place an order for prints. The following steps show how to order prints online using Photoshop Elements.

1. Choose **File | Online Services** to open the Online Services dialog box.

2. Select the online service you want to use, as shown on the following page.

3. Select the desired service.

CHOOSING THE RIGHT PAPER

When you decide to print your digital images, the choice of paper becomes an issue. The plain paper that you use to print out letters and spreadsheets just won't cut it when you print a digital image. The only time you should consider using plain paper to print an image is for testing purposes or to give the nozzles on your printer a workout. Most printer manufacturers have photo-quality paper available for their photo-quality inkjet printers. These papers are designed to work with the manufacturer's printers. You can also find photo-quality paper made by third-party manufacturers, although third-party papers may not give you the desired results.

Many printer manufacturers sell "professional quality" photographic paper. If your printer supports this type of paper and you use it, you can expect more saturated colors, and the look and feel of traditional photographic paper used by camera stores. Another issue with paper is fading. Many printer manufacturers test their papers for light fastness. You can find high-quality papers that will resist fading for up to 72 years.

4. Click **Next** after selecting the desired service. The following image shows the login window for Shutterfly. If you're not a member of Shutterfly, you can join from within the dialog box. Note that you get 15 free prints when you join.

5. After logging in to the online service, follow the prompts to upload your images and order prints.

QUICKFACTS

PRESERVING YOUR PHOTOS

Even if you buy the finest photo-quality paper, your images may still be susceptible to fading, especially if they're in the path of a strong light source, such as unfiltered sunlight beaming in through a window. You can apply what is known as a fixative to your photograph to prevent it from fading. A fixative is a clear, nonglossy coating that protects your photos from harmful ultraviolet rays. You spray the fixative over the print after the ink has dried. Fixatives are available at most art supply stores and many office supply stores.

Create a Photo Book

If you own Photoshop Album 2.0, you can create a photo book. A photo book is a selection of images that are sent to a third-party source for printing and binding. You specify how many images should appear per page as well as the color and fabric of the hardcover binding.

1. Choose **Creations I Photo Book** to open the Choose Your Photo Book Style page, shown next.

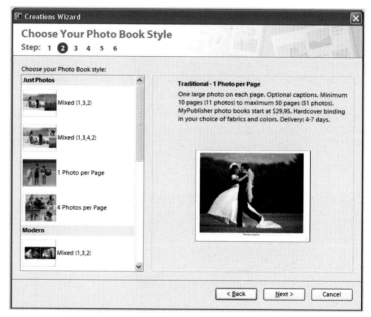

2. Choose the desired style. After you select a style, a description is displayed, along with the minimum price of the photo book.

3. Click **Next** to open the Set Up Your Photo Book page.

4. Type a title, subtitle, and author for your photo book and, if desired, a header and/or footer, as shown on the following page (top illustration). Note that you can also include any captions you've assigned to the photos as well as page numbers.

QUICKFACTS

INVESTIGATING ALTERNATIVE PAPERS

When your skills as a photographer increase, you'll find yourself creating images that warrant special treatment instead of the usual glossy photo-quality paper. As mentioned previously, you can achieve a professional-looking print using heavyweight matte paper. There are also papers on the market that look like canvas, watercolor paper, and so on. When you edit a digital image in Photoshop Elements and give it an artistic quality, printing the photo on one of these papers will make it stand out from a garden-variety photo. Fredrix manufactures a canvas paper, and Arches manufactures a watercolor paper, both of which can be used in an inkjet printer. You can find these papers at fine art supply stores or on the Internet. Type **Arches Inkjet Fine Art Photography Paper** in your favorite search engine. You can find Fredrix Canvas Paper at www.cheapjoes.com. Another source for highly rated fine art and photographic paper is Moab Paper Company at www.moabpaper.com.

5. Click **Next** to open the Pick Your Photos page. Pick your photos as outlined previously in the "Create a Virtual Slide Show" section of this chapter.

6. Click **Next** to reveal the Customize Your Photo Book page. This section of the wizard enables you to preview your photo book. If anything is not to your liking, click the **Back** button to navigate to a previous page of the wizard to change photos, edit the title text, and so on.

7. Click **Next** to reveal the Publish Your Photo Book page.

8. Click the **Online Services** button to reveal the Print Items Using Online Service MyPublisher Print Services dialog box, shown at left.

9. Click **OK** and follow the prompts to upload your images and order your photo book.

high-end features on, 6–7
maintenance tips for, 34
manufacturer websites, 11
needs list for, 8–9
protecting, 98
purchasing, 7–12
reviews on, 10–11
steadying, 74, 75–76
storage media for, 2–4, 12
transferring images from, 7, 101–103
types of, 9–10
digital film, 12
digital image library, 163–177
archiving images in, 172–177
backing up images in, 176–177
batch processing files in, 170–172
contact sheets and, 172–174
deleting images from, 169
File Browser and, 164–172
navigating folders in, 165–166
renaming images in, 170–172
rotating images in, 168–169
sorting images in, 169–170
thumbnails displayed in, 166–167
transferring files in, 177
viewing file details in, 167–168
digital noise, 28, 29, 96
digital photos
archiving, 172–177
composing, 38, 83–91
enhancing, 25
file formats for, 5, 131–132
fixing, 146, 147–148
flash for, 45–47
leveling, 144–145
perspective added to, 88–89
preserving, 214
printing, 210–215
sharing, 179–215
touching up, 140–143
transferring, 7, 101–103, 177
See also images
digital SLRs, 10
cleaning image sensors on, 35
shooting images with, 19–20
digital tablets, 128
digital zoom, 6, 29–30
distortion, lens, 40–41
dog photography, 63–64
downloading images, 7
dreamy images, 44
drop shadows, 155

eCards, 208–210
editing selections, 128

Elliptical Marquee tool, 121, 140–141, 159
elliptical selections, 121
e-mail
eCards sent via, 209–210
optimizing images for, 183–184
sending images via, 184–185
enhancing images, 25
exposure control, 7, 41–42
external flash, 15, 47
external hard drives, 176–177
external storage devices, 15
eyeball icon, 136

family photos. *See* friends and family
fast memory cards, 12
Feather Selection dialog box, 128, 141
File Browser (Photoshop Elements), 110–112, 164–172
batch processing files in, 170–172
deleting images from, 169
launching, 111, 164
menu commands in, 168
navigating folders in, 165–166
renaming images in, 170–172
resizing windows in, 165
rotating images in, 168–169
selecting images in, 112
sorting images in, 169–170
thumbnails displayed in, 166–172
viewing file details in, 167–168
file formats, 5, 131–132
files
backing up, 176–177
batch processing, 170–172
list of recently saved, 184
naming/renaming, 170
transferring between computers, 177
viewing details of, 167–168
See also folders
Fill dialog box, 142, 160
fill flash, 45, 118
Fill Flash command, 118
filling shadows, 93–94
Film Grain layer, 152
filters (camera), 47–48
creating, 49
polarizing, 47, 48
skylight, 35, 48
types of, 48
filters (Photoshop Elements), 156–161
Chalk & Charcoal, 157
Radial Blur, 158–159
Spherize, 160–161
third-party, 160
Filters palette, 156
FireWire ports, 177

fish-eye lens effect, 159–161
fixatives, 214
flash, 45–47
bounce, 46
external, 15, 47
fill, 45
on-camera, 45
portraits and, 62, 92, 93
red-eye reduction, 46
slow synch, 46
Flatten Image command, 143
flattening layers, 143, 144
flowing water, 57
focal length, 41
focusing
auto-focus mode for, 23
depth of field and, 39–40
low-light tip for, 20
off-center subjects and, 23
fog, creating, 44
folders
creating for CD archive, 174
moving images between, 165
navigating in File Browser, 165–166
organizing and naming, 102
web photo gallery, 191
See also files
framing subjects, 91
frequently asked questions (FAQs), 2–7
friends and family, 61–63
digital portraits of, 62
group pictures of, 63
tips on photographing, 61
f-stops, 26–27, 39

Gaussian Blur dialog box, 143
geometric composition, 84–88
circular elements and, 85–86
curves and, 87–88
portrait photography and, 84, 86
rectangles/squares and, 84–85
repeating elements and, 86–87
Get Photos from Files and Folders dialog box, 194
GIF file format, 172, 186
Grain Blur layer, 152
grayscale images, 151–153, 181
greeting cards, 206–207
grid, 144
groups of people, 63

hard drives, 176–177
Help button, 120

optical zoom, 6, 29–30
optimizing images
   for e-mail, 183–184
   for websites, 186–187

P

painterly images, 157
PAL video format, 204
Palette Dock, 134
panning, 71–72
   artistic use of, 81
   blurring backgrounds with, 74–75
paper
   alternative types of, 215
   photo-quality, 210, 213, 215
   scrapbook photo, 206
PDF documents, 208
people pictures
   friends and family, 61–63
   groups of people, 63
   portraits, 62
   public places and, 60–61
   vacation photos and, 59–60
perspective, 88–89
pet photography, 63–64
photo albums, 205–206
photo books, 214–215
Photo Well (Photoshop Album), 198
photographs. *See* digital photos
photo-quality paper, 210, 213, 215
photo-quality printers, 16, 213
Photoshop Album, 179, 192–210
   calendars created in, 199–202
   eCards created in, 208–210
   free starter version of, 192
   greeting cards created in, 206–207
   importing images to, 192–195
   online printing services and, 212–213
   photo albums created in, 205–206
   photo books created in, 214–215
   Photo Well in, 198
   Quick Guide page, 192
   slide shows created in, 195–199
   video CDs created in, 202–205
Photoshop Elements, 105–132
   Batch Processing command, 170–172
   blending modes, 135–138, 147–148
   Clone tool, 146
   color-correcting images in, 113–117
   cropping images in, 129–130
   editing selections in, 128
   File Browser, 110–112, 164–172
   filters, 156–161
   grayscale conversion, 151–153
   launching, 109
   layers used in, 133–140, 147–148
   leveling photos in, 144–145
   lighting adjustments in, 117–118
   monitor calibration and, 105–108
   Motion Blur filter, 149–150
   online printing services and, 212–213
   opacity settings, 138
   opening images in, 109–110
   optimizing images in, 183–184, 186–187
   picture packages, 180–183
   printing photos from, 210–215
   Quick Fix command, 118–120
   Red Eye brush tool, 147–148
   resizing images in, 130, 183, 186
   saving edited images in, 131–132
   selections created in, 120–127
   sending e-mail from, 184–185
   sharpening images in, 113
   Text tool, 153–155
   touching up photos in, 140–143
   Undo History palette, 158
   web photo gallery, 188–191
   Welcome screen, 109
   workspace, 110, 111
Photoshop Elements QuickSteps (Matthews), 115
Photoshop file format, 131
photosites, 2
picture package, 180–183
Picture Package dialog box, 180
pixels, 4
point-and-shoot cameras
   features on, 9–10
   steps for using, 18
polarizing filter, 47, 48, 54
Polygonal Lasso tool, 122–123, 146
Portrait mode, 40
portraits, 62
   framing subjects in, 91
   on-camera flash and, 62, 92, 93
   rule of thirds for, 84
   self-portraits, 65, 66
   window light for, 62, 92–93
pre-focusing, 72
preserving printed photos, 214
preset shooting modes, 24–25
Print Preview dialog box, 210–212
printers, photo-quality, 16, 213
printing digital photos, 210–215
   online services for, 212–213
   paper used for, 210, 213, 215
   photo book creation and, 214–215
   Print Preview option, 210–212
processing RAW images, 104–105
prosumer cameras, 10
purchasing digital cameras, 7–12
   needs list for, 8–9
   news and reviews on, 10–11
   storage media and, 12
   trying before buying, 11
   types of cameras, 9–10

Q

Quality Slider, 184
Quick Fix dialog box, 118–120

R

Radial Blur filter, 158–159
rainstorms, 97, 98
RAW image format, 7
   capturing images in, 49–50
   processing images in, 104–105
RAW viewer utility, 104–105
Recently Saved Files list, 184
rectangular elements, 84–85
Rectangular Marquee tool, 121
rectangular selections, 121
Red Eye brush tool, 147
red-eye
   fixing in Photoshop Elements, 147–148
   reducing when taking photos, 46
Redo button, 117, 120
reflectors, 93–94
   creating makeshift, 99–100
   filling shadows with, 94
remote switch, 93
removable Flash drives, 177
removable storage media, 2–4, 12
   See also memory cards; storage media
renaming image files, 170
repeating elements, 86–87
Resample Image option, 130
Reset button, 117, 120
resizing
   images, 130, 183, 186, 190
   thumbnails, 166–167
resolution
   image, 4
   thumbnail, 173
reviews of digital cameras, 10–11
rotation
   camera, 39
   image, 33, 168–169
Rule of Thirds, 38
   geometric composition and, 84, 85
   portrait photography and, 84, 86

S

Safely Remove Hardware button, 103
Save As dialog box, 131–132, 184
Save command, 131
Save Selection dialog box, 128, 142
saving images, 131–132
scenic vistas, 52–53
scrapbook photo paper, 206
Screen blend mode, 137, 148
seascapes, 55–56

International Contact Information

AUSTRALIA
McGraw-Hill Book Company
Australia Pty. Ltd.
TEL +61-2-9900-1800
FAX +61-2-9878-8881
http://www.mcgraw-hill.com.au
books-it_sydney@mcgraw-hill.com

CANADA
McGraw-Hill Ryerson Ltd.
TEL +905-430-5000
FAX +905-430-5020
http://www.mcgraw-hill.ca

GREECE, MIDDLE EAST, & AFRICA
(Excluding South Africa)
McGraw-Hill Hellas
TEL +30-210-6560-990
TEL +30-210-6560-993
TEL +30-210-6560-994
FAX +30-210-6545-525

MEXICO (Also serving Latin America)
McGraw-Hill Interamericana Editores
S.A. de C.V.
TEL +525-1500-5108
FAX +525-117-1589
http://www.mcgraw-hill.com.mx
carlos_ruiz@mcgraw-hill.com

SINGAPORE (Serving Asia)
McGraw-Hill Book Company
TEL +65-6863-1580
FAX +65-6862-3354
http://www.mcgraw-hill.com.sg
mghasia@mcgraw-hill.com

SOUTH AFRICA
McGraw-Hill South Africa
TEL +27-11-622-7512
FAX +27-11-622-9045
robyn_swanepoel@mcgraw-hill.com

SPAIN
McGraw-Hill/
Interamericana de España, S.A.U.
TEL +34-91-180-3000
FAX +34-91-372-8513
http://www.mcgraw-hill.es
professional@mcgraw-hill.es

UNITED KINGDOM, NORTHERN,
EASTERN, & CENTRAL EUROPE
McGraw-Hill Education Europe
TEL +44-1-628-502500
FAX +44-1-628-770224
http://www.mcgraw-hill.co.uk
emea_queries@mcgraw-hill.com

ALL OTHER INQUIRIES Contact:
McGraw-Hill/Osborne
TEL +1-510-420-7700
FAX +1-510-420-7703
http://www.osborne.com
omg_international@mcgraw-hill.com